simple stitches
EMBROIDERY

39 FAST AND FABULOUS DESIGNS
FOR TODAY'S STITCHER

CAROLINE WARYN

STACKPOLE
BOOKS

Guilford, Connecticut

Published by Stackpole Books
An imprint of The Rowman & Littlefield Publishing Group, Inc.
4501 Forbes Blvd., Ste. 200
Lanham, MD 20706
www.stackpolebooks.com

Distributed by NATIONAL BOOK NETWORK
800-462-6420

Originally published as *Broderie: les techniques pour s'initier*

© 2018 Éditions Eyrolles, Paris, France

www.editions-eyrolles.com

Graphic design: Julie Simoens

Page layout: STDI

All photos of completed embroidery projects are by Camille Riglet © Camille Riglet, except the photo of Leokadia on page 63, which is by the author.

Step-by-step photos: Caroline Waryn

Illustrations of embroidery stitches, pages 9–13, are © Éditions Eyrolles.

The designs in this book were drawn by Marie Savart Illustrations, Camille Isaac Caudrelier, Atelier Sauvage, Frimouss, Charlotte & the Teapot, and Caroline Waryn.

Cover: Studio Eyrolles / photo Camille Riglet

British Library Cataloguing in Publication Information available

Library of Congress Cataloging-in-Publication Data available

Names: Waryn, Caroline, author.
Title: Simple stitches embroidery: 39 fast and fabulous designs for today's stitcher / Caroline Waryn.
Description: Guilford, Connecticut : Stackpole Books, an imprint of The Rowman & Littlefield Publishing Group, Inc., 2020. | Summary: "'Simple Stitches Embroidery' teaches the basics of embroidery, from materials and techniques to the most popular stitches. From adorable elephants for the nursery to cacti for the office and llamas for anywhere, the designs in this book are all easy enough for the beginner"— Provided by publisher.
Identifiers: LCCN 2019057229 (print) | LCCN 2019057230 (ebook) | ISBN 9780811739184 (paperback) | ISBN 9780811769105 (epub)
Subjects: LCSH: Embroidery—Patterns.
Classification: LCC TT771 .W327 2020 (print) | LCC TT771 (ebook) | DDC 746.44—dc23
LC record available at https://lccn.loc.gov/2019057229
LC ebook record available at https://lccn.loc.gov/2019057230

♾️™ The paper used in this publication meets the minimum requirements of American National Standard for Information Sciences—Permanence of Paper for Printed Library Materials, ANSI/NISO Z39.48-1992.

First Edition

simple stitches
EMBROIDERY

ACKNOWLEDGMENTS

A big thank you to Aude, Anne-Lise, and Maria from Éditions Eyrolles, without whom this beautiful adventure would have never come to fruition.

Thanks to the illustrators of this book, who are as talented as they are generous and gave me confidence early on in this project. I am infinitely grateful to you all, Marie, Charlotte, Stéphanie, Clarisse, and Camille.

Thanks to DMC and Perles & Co. for having provided me with the materials necessary to complete this book.

Thanks to my parents, always gracious and attentive. Thank you, Mom, for teaching me how to embroider when I was little and for giving me my first cross-stitch patterns.

Thanks to Nicolas for always being there, for our conversations and your listening ear. You still confuse knitting and embroidery, but you have been living this adventure with me for several years now, and your reassuring presence is important to me.

Thanks to Lucien and Samuel for your energy, your affection, your words—my boys, my first source of inspiration.

CONTENTS

Contents

TOOLS AND TECHNIQUES

MATERIALS NEEDED

Learning to embroider is not that complicated, but it is important to have good tools to work with. The ideal is to put together a little kit so that everything you need is at hand, making it a real pleasure to relax and embroider. Listed below are the materials you will need to make all your projects.

Canvas and Fabric

When starting an embroidery project, the first step is to select the fabric. The fabric is what determines the overall success and look of the work. Though almost all types of cloth can be used for embroidery, opt for fabrics with some weight and that are fairly sturdy. Linen or cotton is ideal for embroidery. But if you wish to use a more fluid fabric, you can attach it to a piece of stabilizer or interfacing to give it some support.

The choice of cloth also depends on the type of embroidery that will be done; some projects require a specific type of cloth. For example, Aida cloth is used for cross-stitch, while even-weave mesh canvas is used for needlepoint.

Tools for Transferring Designs

Once you have selected your piece of cloth, the second step is to transfer your pattern to the fabric. This can be accomplished by various techniques.

- First, get an embroidery transfer pen. The ink from these special pens disappears either upon contact with water or when ironed and allows you to easily trace your design onto the fabric. To do this, place your design, and then your fabric, on a light box or against a window to trace the design. Once you have completed the embroidery, remove all traces of the ink by dipping your embroidered fabric in water for a few seconds or by ironing.

- Water-soluble fabric is very useful when the design to be embroidered is dense and very detailed or is made up of very precise lines that would take too long or be too difficult to trace with a felt-tip pen. In this case, cut a piece of water-soluble stabilizer to the same size as your cloth. Position it on your illustration and trace the illustration onto the water-soluble stabilizer with a ballpoint pen (not a felt-tip). Next, use your embroidery hoop to hold the water-soluble stabilizer tight against your embroidery fabric; this will keep it from moving. Then embroider, inserting your needle through both layers of cloth. Once you have finished the embroidery, soak it in a bowl of warm water for ten minutes, agitating from time to time. The water-soluble stabilizer will completely disappear (as shown in the photo). Finish by holding your embroidery under a stream of water to remove any last traces.

Embroidery Hoops

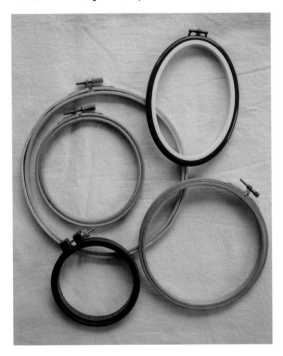

Today, embroidery hoops have become decorative, but let's not forget that they are indispensable tools for embroidery. They are used to stretch the cloth, to hold the water-soluble stabilizer firmly to the fabric to be embroidered, and to keep the thread taut.

Embroidery hoops come in all sizes. They also vary in shape and material, being either round or oval and made of wood or plastic. Always choose a hoop that is larger than your design.

Place your cloth over the inner ring of the hoop with the design in the center. Then put the outer ring over the fabric and press down to hold the fabric between the two rings. Tighten the screw, pulling on your fabric until it is taut. If need be, tighten even more with a screwdriver.

In this book, the size of the hoop to be used is indicated in each pattern. This is for the hoop used when embroidering. It is up to you if you wish to place it in a smaller hoop before hanging it on the wall.

Needles and Scissors

It is also very important to choose the right needle for each project. Be sure that the package you buy says "embroidery needles." They are usually longer and thicker than sewing needles. Before starting, think about matching the size of the needle's eye to the fabric that you will use for the project. If the eye is too big and makes holes in your fabric every time it goes through, switch to the next smaller size.

If you embroider with beads (particularly Miyuki beads), use a beading needle. They are thinner than embroidery needles in order to easily bring the thread through the holes in the beads.

A small pair of sharp, pointed embroidery scissors is also a very good investment. They are indispensable for cutting thread and fabric. Keep them close at hand and do not use them for cutting paper, or they will become dull.

Embroidery Threads

There are several sizes and qualities of embroidery thread or floss. Choose a type that is suitable for the project.

Types of thread vary in packaging (small balls or skeins), in length, in gauge, and in material (cotton, satin/rayon, metallic, etc.).

Floss comes in a huge range of colors. To keep all of your skeins ready to use, keep them in a special organizer box. Wind each color of floss around a small flat cardboard bobbin on which you will note the color reference.

GETTING STARTED

Separating Strands

When using embroidery floss, it is often necessary to first separate the strands. The thread that comes in skeins is usually made up of six strands, which do not have to be used together. In fact, most of the projects in this book are made using only two strands of the thread.

Use this technique to separate the strands:

1 Begin by cutting the floss to a length of no more than 16 in. (40 cm).

2 Then hold one of the ends of the thread between two fingers.

3 Turn the thread in the opposite direction of the twist; the six strands should separate naturally.

4 Take the desired number of strands and pull gently to separate them from the rest.

NOTE

IF THE NUMBER OF STRANDS IS NOT SPECIFIED IN THE PATTERN DIRECTIONS, USE TWO STRANDS OF FLOSS FOR YOUR EMBROIDERY.

Starting Your Project

The first thing to do is to cut a piece of thread no longer than 16 in. (40 cm). If you opt to cut it longer than that, the thread is more likely to become tangled and knotted. Next, separate the number of strands required for the pattern, as explained previously. Then thread the needle.

You can then make a small knot at the end of the thread and begin to embroider. But if you want your embroidery project to be neat and tidy on the back side, without the bumps made by knots, you can also secure your thread in the following manner:

1 Cut only one strand of the floss and fold it in half.

2 Thread the two cut ends of the floss into the eye of the needle.

3 Insert your needle from the back side to the front side of your cloth; then, with two fingers on the back side, hold on to the small loop at the end of the thread.

4 Once the stitch is finished, bring your needle through this little loop and pull the thread.

This is the most effective way to begin.

Keeping Threads on Hold

Some embroidery projects require several colors of thread. You can use a technique to keep your threads on hold so you don't have to cut and secure the threads each time there is a color change.

1 Insert your needle from the back to the front of your fabric, keeping it far from your design.

2 Remove the needle and hold the thread on the front side with the hand that is holding the hoop.

3 Make a small slipknot at the end of the thread that you can easily unknot to continue using the color later in the project.

You can now go on to another color and then come back to this first color of floss by again threading it on your needle when needed.

Finishing Steps

When you have finishing embroidering with one of your threads, you must secure it so your stitches do not come out. Take your needle to the back side of the work and run it under a few stitches, and then clip the thread flush with the fabric.

1 When your embroidered design is finished, remove it from the hoop.

2 Remove all traces of the pattern by dipping the fabric in water to dissolve the water-soluble stabilizer or to wash away the ink.

3 Let your work dry. You can then put it back in its original hoop or in a slightly larger hoop to let it dry while taut.

4 Once it is dry, iron your work if needed. This is a delicate process, and several precautions should be taken. Sometimes it is adequate to let the fabric dry taut in the hoop, but if this is not the case, then choose the damp pressing cloth method: Never place the iron directly on the embroidery thread. Dampen a cloth and place it on your piece of embroidery. Press while keeping this cloth between your embroidery and the iron without using steam.

5 If you wish to keep your finished piece in a hoop, place it in the hoop as previously explained.

After ensuring that the fabric is stretched uniformly taut, tighten the screw, using a screwdriver if necessary. It will not look good if the fabric is too tight on one side, distorting the design. Once it is positioned properly, you can cut your fabric flush with the hoop and hang it that way.

STITCH GUIDE

Backstitch

This stitch is used quite often to make straight and curved lines. Comprising a series of stitches placed one right after the other, it is always worked from right to left. It is the hoop that turns, not your stitches!

See the Mountain pattern, page 18, for more detailed directions on how to work this stitch.

Straight Stitch

This stitch can be horizontal, vertical, or diagonal and can be used to cover a large area when repeated several times.

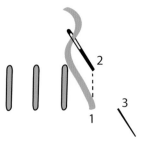

Stem Stitch

Used for lines, curves, and flower stems, this stitch is always worked from left to right.

See the Mountain pattern, page 16, for more detailed directions on how to work this stitch.

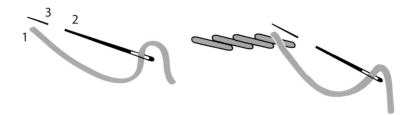

Long and Short Satin Stitch

This stitch is used to fill spaces. By alternating short and long straight stitches, it gives texture to the embroidery.

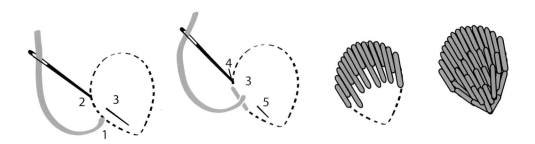

French Knot

The French knot is very decorative and is used to give your embroidery texture and depth.
See the Miniatures pattern, page 85, for more detailed directions on how to work this stitch.

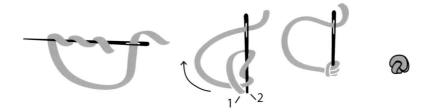

Woven Circle

This stitch starts with a star made of five or seven radiating stitches and somewhat resembles a rose. When working this stitch, make sure that all the radiating stitches or arms are the same length. All of the depth comes from the way the spaces between those arms of the star are filled, by bringing the needle and thread first over and then under each arm until the space is completely covered.

See the Love of a Lifetime pattern, page 74, for more detailed directions on how to work this stitch.

Cross-Stitch

Cross-stitch is a separate branch of embroidery. For a long time, it was very popular, and many thought that embroidery was limited to this stitch. Cross-stitch embroidery is the transcription of a diagram to a fabric where each colored square on the diagram becomes one embroidered cross-stitch. All of these small crosses placed one next to the other create a design, somewhat like pixels.

To make a half cross-stitch, also used in embroidery, simply complete only half of the stitch.

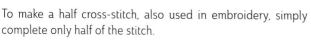

See the Skull pattern, page 55, for more detailed directions on how to work the half cross-stitch.

Chain Stitch

This is a very pretty stitch that looks like a series of small loops. It gives a textured effect and can be very practical when used on clothing; it can also be made to look like lace.

Fishbone Stitch

This stitch is used mainly to embroider the inside of leaves. It is a series of straight stitches that cross over one another in order to fill a motif.

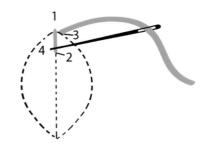

Star Stitch

This stitch is comprised of a regular cross-stitch with an upright cross-stitch worked directly on top of it. It has a pretty texture that makes it very practical for making borders.

See the Skull pattern, page 56, for more detailed directions on how to work this stitch.

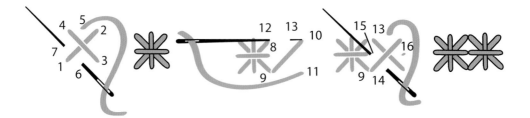

Fly Stitch

This stitch is often used when embroidering leaves; it can be used to make the veins.

See the Leokadia pattern, page 67, for more detailed directions on how to work this stitch.

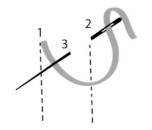
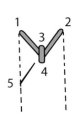

Detached Chain Stitch

This stitch is used to make flowers.

See the Leokadia pattern, page 65, for more detailed directions on how to work this stitch.

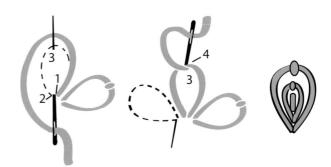

RECOMMENDATIONS

Thread

This book works mainly with DMC threads.

DMC offers a large choice of threads, colors, and textures that you will find at many retailers but also at its online store: www.dmc.com/us/.

High-quality silk thread is gorgeous when used in embroidery. The store Au Ver à Soie (Silk House) sells beautiful thread. It can be purchased at the store or through its website: www.auverasoie.com.

Fabric

Any type of fabric can be embroidered. I very much like to embroider on linen. It comes in many colors, is a beautiful quality, and is very easy to work with. I also buy my water-soluble stabilizer cut to order.

Hoops, Beads, Pens

For these accessories, you will find a wide selection online and in your local craft store.

MOUNTAIN

Illustration by Camille Isaac Caudrelier

The different stitches used in this project create its texture and depth; we use the same thread for the entire design.

MATERIALS

- Linen, 12 x 12 in. (30 x 30 cm)
- 10 in. (25 cm) embroidery hoop
- Embroidery needle
- Embroidery pen

STITCHES USED

- Stem stitch (p. 10)
- Straight stitch (p. 10)
- Backstitch (p. 9)

THREAD USED

DMC 6-Strand Cotton Embroidery Floss

310

TIP

TO EMBROIDER LINES THAT ARE STRAIGHT AND PARALLEL, ALWAYS INSERT THE NEEDLE IN THE SAME WEFT ROW OF THE FABRIC. THE WEFT BECOMES A VISUAL INDICATOR. BE SURE TO MAKE THE STITCHES THE SAME LENGTH AS WELL.

STEM STITCH

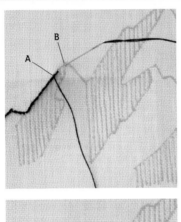

Bring your needle up at point A and insert it into point B on the right side of your work.

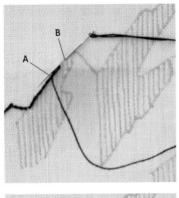

Then bring the needle up again on the right side midway between points A and B.

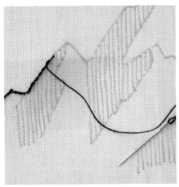

Repeat these steps, following the lines of the pattern.

✕ INSTRUCTIONS

1 Transfer the illustration onto your fabric with the embroidery pen and place the fabric in your hoop.

2 Work the contours of the mountains in stem stitch.

3 Work the trees and the birds in straight stitch.

4 Work the parallel lines in backstitch.

5 Embroider the word "mountain" in backstitch.

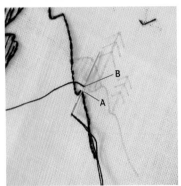

Insert your needle at point A going toward point B on the right side of your work, following the line on your pattern.

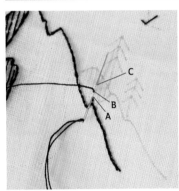

Bring the needle up ⅛ of an inch (3 mm) or so farther at point C, still on the pattern line drawn on your fabric.

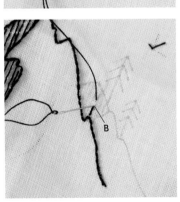

Then go down again at point B. Repeat as above to backstitch the lines.

Mountain

MOUNTAIN

This template is shown at 80 percent of
its actual size. If you wish to embroider
it as is, use a 10 in. (25 cm) hoop.

MY TROPICAL GARDEN

Illustration by Frimouss

It is calming to embroider plants. You can play with nuances of green, bring in touches of color, or instead choose neutral tones. This illustration lends itself perfectly to the urban jungle atmosphere so popular in interior design.

MATERIALS

- Linen, 14 in. x 20 in. (35 x 50 cm)
- 12 in. (30 cm) embroidery hoop
- Embroidery needle
- Embroidery pen

STITCHES USED

- Straight stitch (p. 10)
- Stem stitch (p. 10)
- Backstitch (p. 9)
- Long and short satin stitch (p. 10)
- French knot (p. 11)

THREAD USED

DMC Pearl Cotton size 5

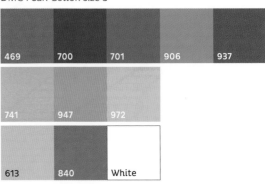

469 · 700 · 701 · 906 · 937
741 · 947 · 972
613 · 840 · White

DMC Pearl Cotton size 8

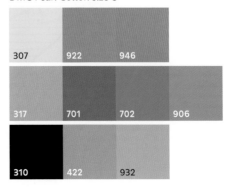

307 · 922 · 946
317 · 701 · 702 · 906
310 · 422 · 932

The numbers indicated in this illustration correspond to the numbers in parentheses found in the instructions.

× INSTRUCTIONS

1 Transfer the illustration onto your fabric with the embroidery pen and place the fabric in your hoop.

2 Work the leaves (1) in straight stitch with DMC pearl cotton size 8 color 702. Vary the direction of the stitch on each leaf so the light hits each leaf differently.

3 Work the lemons (2) in straight stitch with DMC pearl cotton size 8 color 307.

4 Work the trunk and the branches (3) in stem stitch with DMC pearl cotton size 5 color 840.

5 Work the outlines of the pot (4) in stem stitch with DMC pearl cotton size 8 color 922.

6 Work the interior spaces of the pot (5) in straight stitch with DMC pearl cotton size 5 color 947.

7 Work the top and bottom of the second pot (6) in straight stitch with DMC pearl cotton size 5 color 613.

8 Work the center of the pot (7) and the inside of the diamonds (31) in straight stitch with the white DMC pearl cotton size 5.

9 Work the circles in the center of the diamonds (8) and the two stripes (10) on the pot in straight stitch with DMC pearl cotton size 5 color 741. Then work the outline of the diamonds (8) in backstitch with the same thread.

10 Work the handle (9) in straight stitch with DMC pearl cotton size 5 color 840.

11 Work the background of the third pot (11) in straight stitch with DMC pearl cotton size 5 color 613.

12 For the monstera leaf (12), work the edge in straight stitch with DMC pearl cotton size 5 color 906 and the inside in straight stitch with DMC pearl cotton size 5 color 701.

13 Work the top and bottom of the third pot (13) in straight stitch with DMC pearl cotton size 5 color 741.

14 For the tail of the toucan (14), work the outline in backstitch with DMC pearl cotton size 8 color 310 and the inside in straight stitch with DMC pearl cotton size 8 color 317.

15 Work the lower part of the fourth pot (15) in straight stitch with DMC pearl cotton size 5 color 937.

16 Work the upper part of the pot (16) in straight stitch with DMC pearl cotton size 5 color 741.

17 Work the feathers overhanging the tail (17) in straight stitch with the white DMC pearl cotton size 5.

18 Work the edge of the toucan's wing (18) in straight stitch with DMC pearl cotton size 8 color 922.

19 Work the bands of the haworthia (19) in straight stitch with DMC pearl cotton size 5 color 700.

20 Work the inside of the leaves and the edges of the plant (20) in straight stitch with DMC pearl cotton size 8 color 906.

21 Work the body of the toucan in long and short satin stitch with DMC pearl cotton size 8 color 310. Then make its eye with a French knot using the same thread.

22 Work the toucan's face (22) in straight stitch with the white DMC pearl cotton size 5.

23 Work the leaves of the banana tree (23) in straight stitch with DMC pearl cotton size 8 color 702. Vary the direction of the stitch on each leaf so the light hits each stitch differently.

24 Work the trunk of the banana tree (24) in long and short satin stitch with DMC pearl cotton size 8 color 422.

25 Work the toucan's beak (25) in straight stitch with DMC pearl cotton size 5 color 972.

26 Work the end of the beak (26) in straight stitch with DMC pearl cotton size 8 color 946.

27 Work the outline of the cactus (27) and the spines in stem stitch with DMC pearl cotton size 5 color 469.

28 Work the inside of the cactus (28) in short and long satin stitch with DMC pearl cotton size 8 color 701.

29 Work the handle of the third pot (29) in straight stitch with DMC pearl cotton size 8 color 922.

30 Work the legs of the toucan (30) in straight stitch with DMC pearl cotton size 8 color 932.

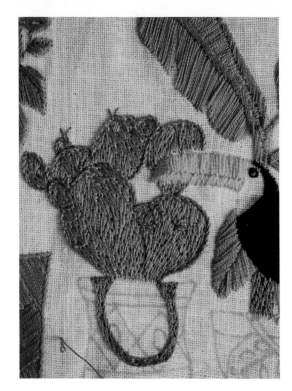

VARIATION: MY LITTLE JUNGLE

×

Illustrations by Frimouss

Green and tropical themes are often featured today in interior design, so don't hesitate to make yourself a little collection of embroidered miniatures. You can cover one of your walls with these very colorful plant-inspired little hoops. Stéphanie (alias Frimouss) brings us five designs, just as enjoyable to look at as they are to embroider!

MATERIALS

- Linen, 6 x 6 in. (15 x 15 cm) for each illustration
- Water-soluble stabilizer
- 6 in. (15 cm) embroidery hoop
- Embroidery needle

STITCHES USED

- Backstitch (p. 9)
- Long and short satin stitch (p. 10)
- Straight stitch (p. 10)
- French knot (p. 11)
- Stem stitch (p. 10)

THREAD USED

DMC 6-Strand Cotton Embroidery Floss

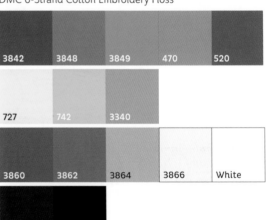

| 3842 | 3848 | 3849 | 470 | 520 |

| 727 | 742 | 3340 |

| 3860 | 3862 | 3864 | 3866 | White |

| 09 | 310 |

DMC Pearl Cotton size 5

| 909 |

Toucan

1 Transfer the illustration onto the water-soluble stabilizer and hold it firmly against the fabric with the hoop.

2 Work the outline of the body and the tail in backstitch with DMC cotton floss color 310.

3 Work the inside of the body in long and short satin stitch with the same floss.

4 Work the inside of the tail in straight stitch with the white DMC cotton floss.

5 Work the outline of the legs and claws in backstitch with DMC cotton floss color 3860.

6 Work the inside of the legs in straight stitch with the white DMC cotton floss.

7 Make the eye with a French knot using DMC cotton floss color 310.

8 Work the head in straight stitch with the white DMC cotton floss.

9 To make the beak, work the bottom of the beak in straight stitch with DMC cotton floss color 727, the end with color 3340, and the top with color 742. For each part, first work the outline in backstitch.

Bean

1 Transfer the illustration onto the water-soluble stabilizer and hold it firmly against the fabric with the hoop.

2 Work the outline of the leaf and the veins in stem stitch with DMC cotton floss color 3848.

3 Work the inside of the leaf in straight stitch with DMC cotton floss color 3849.

4 Work the outlines of the bean in stem stitch with DMC cotton floss color 09. Work the shell with the same thread in straight stitch.

5 Work the inside of the bean in straight stitch: the shell with DMC cotton floss color 3862 and the center with color 3864.

6 Work the seeds in straight stitch with DMC cotton floss color 310.

TIP

THIS BEAN CAN EASILY BE TRANSFORMED INTO A LEMON OR A KIWI SIMPLY BY CHANGING THE COLORS OF THE FLOSS.

Banana Tree

1 Transfer the illustration onto the water-soluble stabilizer and hold it firmly against the fabric with the hoop.

2 Work the outline of the stem and leaves in stem stitch with DMC cotton floss color 3848.

3 Work the inside of the stem and leaves in straight stitch with DMC cotton floss color 3849. Vary the direction of the stitch on each leaf as often as possible to play up the reflected sheen of the floss and give real depth to the plant.

4 Work the handle in backstitch with DMC cotton floss color 3862 and add a French knot for the handle attachment using the same thread.

5 Make the pot with the stripes worked in straight stitch, alternating DMC cotton floss colors 3842 and 3866.

NOTE

✕

THE DIRECTION OF THE STITCHES AND THE SHEEN FROM THE FLOSS GIVE DEPTH TO THE EMBROIDERY.

Prickly Pear Cactus

1 Transfer the illustration onto the water-soluble stabilizer and hold it firmly against the fabric with the hoop.

2 Work the spines in straight stitch with DMC pearl cotton size 5 color 909.

3 Work the outline of the cactus in stem stitch with DMC cotton floss color 520; then work the inside in long and short satin stitch in color 470.

4 For the handle of the bag, use DMC cotton floss color 3842, working the edges in stem stitch and the inside in straight stitch.

5 For the different sections of the bag, work the outline in backstitch and the inside in straight stitch with the colors shown on the next page.

1. 3862   2. 3866   3. 3864

Haworthia

1 Transfer the illustration onto the water-soluble stabilizer and hold it firmly against the fabric with the hoop.

2 Work the outline of the leaves in stem stitch with DMC cotton floss color 3849.

3 Work the inside in straight stitch using DMC pearl cotton size 5 color 909 for the bands and DMC cotton floss color 3849 for the leaves.

4 Work the outline of the pot in stem stitch and the inside in long and short satin stitch with DMC cotton floss color 3866.

5 Make the dots in French knot stitch with DMC cotton floss color 3842.

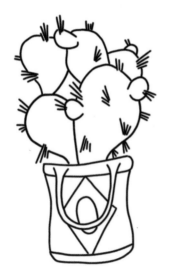

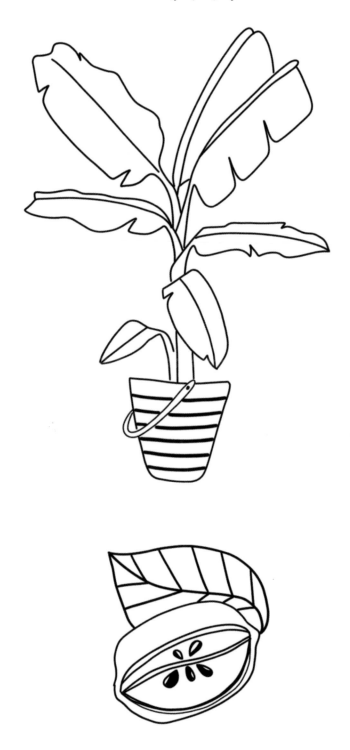

WILD WOMAN

Illustration by Atelier Sauvage

This minimalist design by Clarisse (a.k.a. Atelier Sauvage) is a veritable playground for the imagination. This motif can be embroidered in many ways, and each of them will make it unique. One option is to trace the design in black with a little touch of color on the lips and some carefully selected colors, or you could opt for an explosion of colors for the flowers. Here is where we can play with the threads like a painter plays with a palette!

MATERIALS

- Linen, 16 x 16 in.
  (40 × 40 cm)
- Water-soluble stabilizer
- 14 in. (35.6 cm)
  embroidery hoop
- Embroidery needle

STITCHES USED

- Backstitch (p. 9)
- Straight stitch (p. 10)
- French knot (p. 11)
- Stem stitch (p. 10)

THREAD USED

DMC 6-Strand Cotton Embroidery Floss

DMC Pearl Cotton size 5

The numbers indicated in this illustration correspond to the numbers in parentheses found in the instructions.

✕ INSTRUCTIONS

1 Transfer the illustration onto the water-soluble stabilizer and hold it firmly against the fabric with the hoop.

2 To make the two large flowers (1), work the outline of the petals and the center of the flowers in backstitch with DMC cotton floss color 22, and work the lines inside in backstitch with DMC cotton floss color 21.

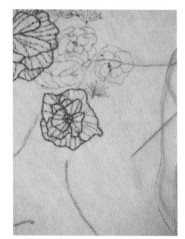

3 Work the lips in straight stitch with DMC cotton floss color 22.

4 Work the leaf (2) in backstitch with DMC cotton floss color 3848.

5 Work the flower (3) in backstitch with DMC cotton floss color 3852.

6 Work the leaves and flowers (4) in backstitch with DMC cotton floss color 28.

7 Work the flowers (5) in backstitch with DMC cotton floss color 29.

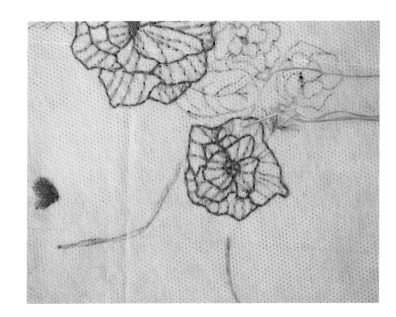

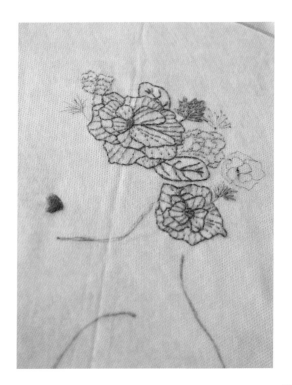

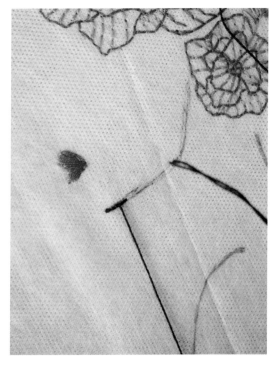

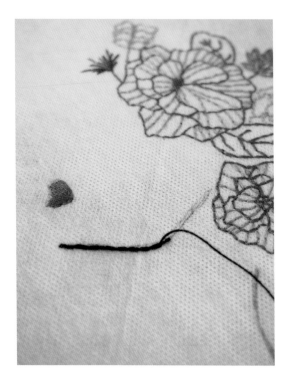

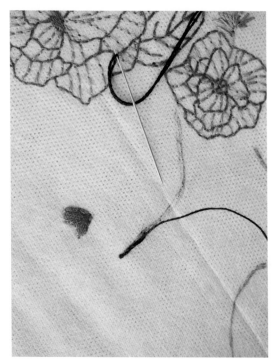

8 Make the flower (6), working the stems in backstitch and the buds in French knot with DMC cotton floss color 21.

9 Work the leaves (7) in backstitch with DMC cotton floss color 3847.

10 Work the woman's body in stem stitch with DMC pearl cotton size 5 color 310.

ARCHIBALD PIN

Illustration by the author

Small crosses, shiny thread, a bit of felt, a pin back, a few hours of work—nothing more is needed to adopt this little crowned panda with a look that is totally kawaii. Once embroidered, you will no longer be able to go without your pretty little Archibald pin!

MATERIALS

- Aida cloth, 12 x 12 in.
  (30 x 30 cm)
- Felt
- Double-sided fusible
  webbing
- Embroidery needle
- 2 black Miyuki beads
- Safety catch pin back
- Fabric or jewelry glue

STITCHES USED

- Cross-stitch (p. 11)
- Backstitch (p. 9)
- Straight stitch (p. 10)

THREAD USED

DMC 6-Strand Cotton Embroidery Floss

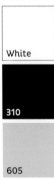

White

310

605

DMC Diamant Metallic Thread

D301

✕ INSTRUCTIONS

1 Follow the diagram, working a cross-stitch for each square and following the color coding. Work the crown in DMC Diamant metallic thread color D301, the cheeks in DMC cotton floss color 605, and the rest in DMC cotton floss color 310.

2 Work the inside of the head and the eyes with the white DMC cotton floss.

3 Sew on two black Miyuki beads for the eyes.

4 When the embroidery is completed, iron with a damp pressing cloth.

5 Trim the fabric around the embroidered motif to make a small square.

NOTE
✕
THE CHEEKS CAN ALSO BE
WORKED IN BACKSTITCH.

6 Cut out a square of the same size in both the felt and the double-sided fusible webbing.

7 Place the fusible webbing between the wrong side of the embroidery and the felt. Then, with a hot iron, press the embroidery to the felt.

8 Cut the fabric around the head of the panda, leaving a margin of about $1/8$ to $3/16$ in. (3 to 5 mm).

9 Finish by working straight stitches all around the edge of the pin (as shown in the photo) or work a blanket stitch for a more polished finish.

10 Glue the pin backing to the wrong side of the embroidery with fabric or jewelry glue. Let dry for several hours before wearing your handiwork.

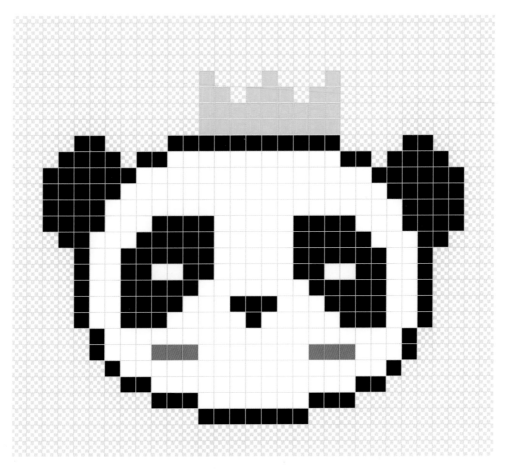

MY EMBROIDERED WORDS

Illustrations by the author

Embroidering a saying or a little love note and giving it framed in a hoop, or putting it on a young child's clothing, a tote bag, or a pencil case, is so easy to do that you'll immediately want to make more!

MATERIALS

- Linen, 16 x 16 in. (40 x 40 cm) and 8 x 8 in. (20 x 20 cm)
- 14 in. (35 cm) and 7 in. (18 cm) embroidery hoops
- Embroidery needle
- Embroidery pen

STITCHES USED

- Straight stitch (p.10)
- Backstitch (p. 9)
- Chain stitch (p. 12)
- French knot (p. 11)
- Stem stitch (p. 10)

THREAD USED

DMC 6-Strand Cotton Embroidery Floss

3799   3842

726

DMC Pearl Cotton size 5

352

518

DMC Pearl Cotton size 8

959

You Are the Sunshine of My Life

1 Transfer the illustration onto the 16 x 16 in. (40 x 40 cm) fabric with the embroidery pen and place it in the 14 in. (35 cm) hoop.

2 Work the crown of leaves in straight stitch with DMC pearl cotton size 5 color 518.

3 Embroider the word "Sunshine" with DMC pearl cotton size 5 color 352, working the edge of the letters in backstitch. Some parts of the letters are thicker and will need to be filled in with straight stitch.

4 Work all the other words in backstitch with DMC pearl cotton size 8 color 959 except for the Y in "You" and the L in "Life," which are worked in chain stitch. Make the dot over the "i" with a French knot.

5 Work the waves in backstitch with one strand from a skein of DMC cotton embroidery floss color 3842.

6 Work the sun in backstitch with DMC cotton floss color 726.

Messy but Happy Family

1 Transfer the illustration onto the 8 x 8 in. (20 x 20 cm) fabric with the embroidery pen and place it in the 7 in. (18 cm) hoop.

2 Work the leaves and the word "but" in backstitch with DMC embroidery floss color 3799.

3 Work the word "Family" in chain stitch with DMC embroidery floss color 3799.

4 Embroider the words "Messy" and "Happy" in stem stitch with DMC embroidery floss color 3799. Fill out the thicker parts of these letters as needed with straight stitch.

SKULL

Illustration by the author

If I say the word "needlepoint," you undoubtedly think of something like an old picture of a deer at the edge of a lake—a decorative item that is a bit out of style. Yet an updated woven finish gives needlepoint a boho chic look. A well-made design, some fringe to finish it off, and you'll never look at needlepoint in the same way again!

MATERIALS

- Canvas, 20 x 20 in.
  (50 x 50 cm)
- Embroidery needle
- Strip of wood or a branch

STITCHES USED

- Half cross-stitch (p. 11)
- Star stitch (p. 12)

THREAD USED

Sport weight wool or cotton yarn

Beige

Charcoal gray

Light gray

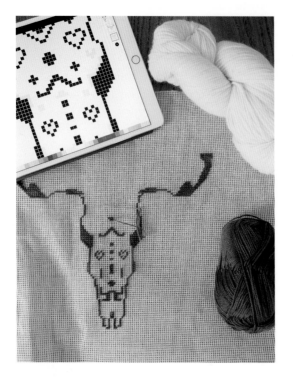

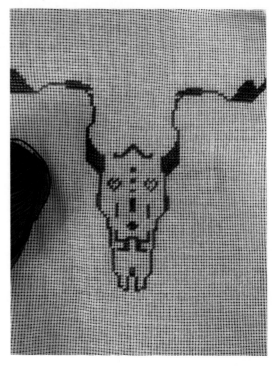

✕ INSTRUCTIONS

1 Following the diagram and color coding, work a half cross-stitch in each square.

2 Finish by working a border in star stitch to give some depth to your needlework.

HALF CROSS-STITCH

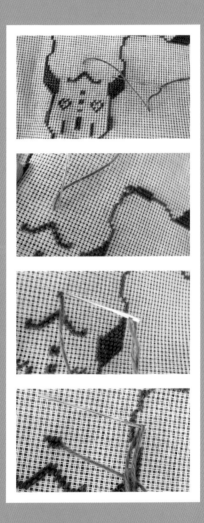

Bring the needle up through the canvas . . .

. . . and work a diagonal stitch to produce a short, slanted line.

Work all the stitches in the same direction. Turn canvas to work the next row.

TIP

×

AS PART OF THE CANVAS WILL NOT BE EMBROIDERED (UNLESS YOU WANT TO EMBROIDER THE BACKGROUND AS WELL), BE SURE THE THREADS STAY BEHIND THE DESIGN AND DO NOT CROSS THE AREA OF THE CANVAS THAT IS NOT EMBROIDERED. IT WOULD BE A SHAME AND UNATTRACTIVE TO SEE THREADS RUNNING BEHIND THE CANVAS.

STAR STITCH

×

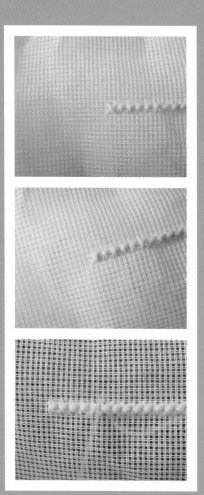

Start by embroidering a
cross-stitch.

- -

Then make a vertical stitch that
crosses over the center of this X.

- -

Next make a horizontal stitch that
crosses over the center of the
cross-stitch.

FINISHING

×

IRON WITH A DAMP PRESSING CLOTH. CUT THE CANVAS AROUND YOUR EMBROIDERY
AND GLUE A STRIP OF WOOD TO THE TOP OF YOUR CANVAS. FINALLY, ATTACH FRINGE
TO THE BOTTOM EDGE.

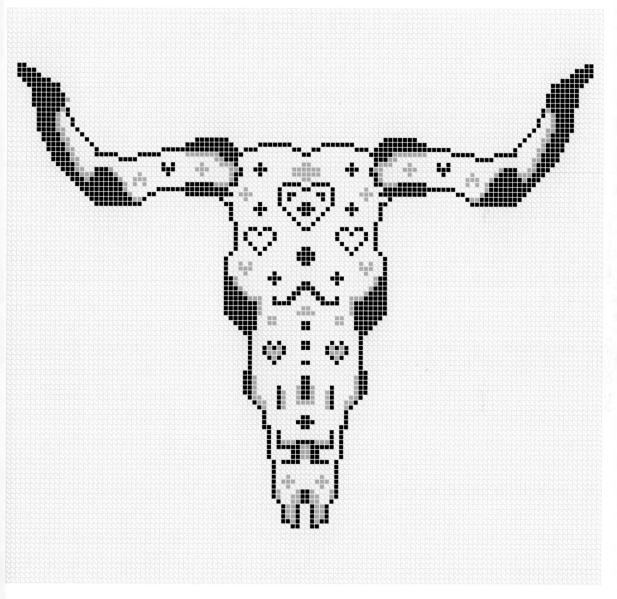

MIMOSAS

Illustration by the author

Mimosas bring sunshine and softness into the house. Embroider a few branches and give depth to the flowers with French knots.

MATERIALS

- Linen, 12 x 12 in.
  (30 x 30 cm)
- 10 in. (25 cm) embroidery
  hoop
- Embroidery pen
- Embroidery needle

STITCHES USED

- Stem stitch (p. 10)
- Straight stitch (p. 10)
- French knot (p. 11)

THREAD USED

DMC 6-Strand Cotton Embroidery Floss

726

991

3863

× INSTRUCTIONS

1 Transfer the illustration onto your fabric with the embroidery pen and place it in the hoop.

2 Work the branches in stem stitch with DMC embroidery floss color 3863.

3 Work the leaves in straight stitch with DMC embroidery floss color 991.

4 Make the mimosa flowers, filling in the circles with French knots worked close together using DMC embroidery floss color 726.

LEOKADIA

Illustration by the author

Leokadia was my maternal grandmother's first name. Even though she spent her entire life in France, she always kept her native Poland in her heart. With this design, I wanted to pay tribute to the traditional embroidery of Eastern Europe with a profusion of colors and motifs.

MATERIALS

- Linen, 12 x 12 in. (30 x 30 cm)
- Water-soluble stabilizer
- 10 in. (25 cm) embroidery hoop
- Embroidery needle
- Beading needle
- Miyuki bugle or tube beads

STITCHES USED

- Straight stitch (p. 10)
- Backstitch (p. 9)
- Fly stitch (p. 12)
- French knot (p. 11)
- Detached chain stitch (p. 13)

THREAD USED

DMC Six-Strand Cotton Embroidery Floss

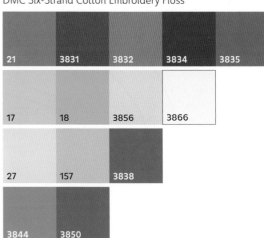

DMC Pearl Cotton size 5

NOTE

✕

THIS DESIGN IS COMPLETELY SYMMETRICAL. EVERY MOTIF MUST THEREFORE BE EMBROIDERED THE SAME WAY ON BOTH SIDES OF THE WORK.

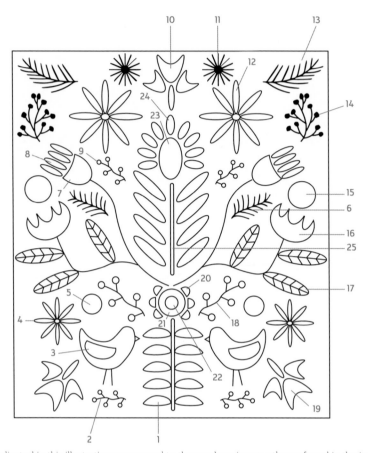

The numbers indicated in this illustration correspond to the numbers in parentheses found in the instructions.

✕ INSTRUCTIONS

1 Transfer the illustration onto the water-soluble stabilizer and hold it firmly against the fabric with the hoop.

2 Work the stem and leaves (1) in straight stitch with DMC cotton floss color 3850.

3 For the little sprig (2), work the stem in backstitch and the circles in French knot with DMC cotton floss color 3856.

4 Work the bird (3) in straight stitch, the wings with DMC cotton floss color 21, the body with DMC cotton floss color 27, and then the beak and legs with DMC cotton floss color 3832.

5 Work the flower (4) in detached chain stitch with DMC cotton floss color 3832.

6 Work the sprigs (6) in straight stitch with DMC cotton floss color 3834.

7 Work the base (7) and petals (8) of the flower in straight stitch, using DMC cotton floss color 3856 for the base (7) and DMC cotton floss color 3844 for the petals (8).

DETACHED CHAIN STITCH

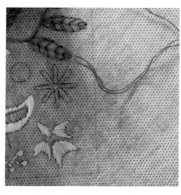

Bring your needle up at one side of the base of a petal, and then insert it again at the other side of the base of that petal. Don't pull the thread all the way through.

Bring your needle up at the outside end of the petal.

Then pull the thread gently, forming a loop, keeping your thread inside that loop. Next, insert your needle right next to where you came up but on the outer side of the loop.

8 Work roses in the circles (5) in woven circle stitch with DMC pearl cotton size 5 color 157.

9 Make the little sprigs of fruit (9), working the stem in backstitch and the circles in French knot with DMC cotton floss color 3831.

10 Work the top center motif (10) in straight stitch with DMC cotton floss color 18. Work the similar motifs (19) in the same way.

11 Work the flowers (11) in straight stitch with DMC cotton floss color 3831.

12 Work the flowers (12) in detached chain stitch with DMC cotton floss color 3832.

13 Work the sprigs (13) in straight stitch with DMC cotton floss color 3835.

14 For the branches (14), work the stem in backstitch with DMC cotton floss color 3838 and the circles in French knot with DMC cotton floss color 3866.

15 Work a rose in the circles (15) in woven circle stitch with DMC pearl cotton color 760.

FLY STITCH

Bring your thread up on one end of a vein and then down on the other end.

Bring the needle up in the center, in line with that vein and inside the loop of thread.

Gently pull up the thread.

Insert the needle down over the loop a short distance below that, and repeat steps to form a stem.

16 Work the petals (16 and 24) in straight stitch with DMC cotton floss color 3838.

17 Work the stems and outside edges of the leaves (17) in straight stitch with DMC cotton floss color 3850. Work the veins of the leaves in fly stitch with the same floss.

18 For the larger sprigs of fruit (18), work the stem in backstitch and the circles in French knot with DMC cotton floss color 3856.

19 Work the floral motifs (20, 21, 22, and 23) in straight stitch with DMC cotton floss color 17 (20), color 3835 (21), and color 21 (22 and 23).

20 Embroider the large center stem (25) with DMC cotton floss color 18, working the stem in stem stitch and the leaves in straight stitch.

21 Stitch the tube beads to the border around your embroidery. Bring up your needle to the right of the bead placement, thread the bead, and then bring the needle down again as close as possible to the previous bead.

LOVE OF A LIFETIME

✕

Illustration by Marie Savart Illustrations

This illustration, full of sweetness and whimsy, is the ideal gift for a new baby.
You could leave your finished work in the embroidery hoop and give it like that to decorate
the baby's room, or perhaps you could use this design to customize a diaper bag or
decorate a swaddle blanket.

MATERIALS

- Linen, 16 x 16 in.
  (40 x 40 cm)
- Water-soluble stabilizer
- 12 in. (30 cm) embroidery
  hoop
- Embroidery needle

STITCHES USED

- Backstitch (p. 9)
- Stem stitch (p. 10)
- Chain stitch (p. 12)
- Straight stitch (p. 10)
- Woven circle (p. 11)
- French knot (p. 11)

THREAD USED

DMC Six-Strand Cotton Embroidery Floss

3832	3835

16	17	3853

535	3839	3842	3846	3848

DMC Pearl Cotton size 5

352

DMC Diamant Metallic Thread

D301

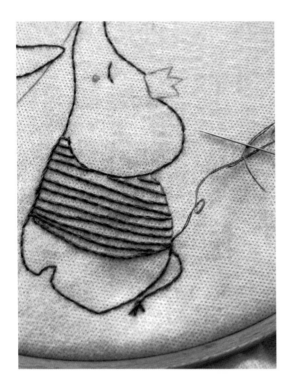

× INSTRUCTIONS

1 Transfer the illustration onto the water-soluble stabilizer and hold it firmly against the fabric with the hoop.

2 Work the elephants' eyes and the outlines of their bodies in backstitch with DMC cotton floss color 535.

3 Work the Breton shirt on the papa elephant in stem stitch with DMC cotton floss color 3842.

4 Work the Breton shirt on the mama elephant with DMC cotton floss color 3832. Work the outside lines in backstitch and the stripes in chain stitch.

5 Make the baby's shirt with DMC cotton floss color 3848, working the outside edges in backstitch and the stripes in stem stitch.

> ── N O T E ──
> ×
> WORK ALL THE CHAIN
> STITCHES IN THE SAME
> DIRECTION, SO THE
> STITCHES ARE GOING THE
> SAME WAY ON EACH STRIPE.

The numbers indicated in this illustration correspond to the numbers in parentheses found in the instructions.

6 Embroider the crown of flowers on the mama elephant.

– Work the leaves (1) in straight stitch with DMC cotton floss color 3848.
– Work the top branch (2) in backstitch with DMC cotton floss color 3839.
– Work the lower branch (3) with DMC cotton floss color 3835. Work the stems in backstitch and the flowers in French knot.

– Work the middle branch (5) with DMC cotton floss color 3853. Work the stems in backstitch and the flowers in French knot.
– Work the last branches (6), the flowers in French knot and the stems in straight stitch, with DMC cotton floss color 17.
– Make a few straight stitches to the right of the flowers (7) with DMC Diamant metallic thread color D301.

WOVEN CIRCLE

Bring your needle up in the center of the circle, and then form a star with five radiating stitches, making sure these stitches are evenly spaced.

- -

Bring your needle and thread up near the center and weave it clockwise under and over each of the radiating stitches until the circle is completely filled.

- -

NOTE

×

THE WOVEN CIRCLE GIVES REAL DEPTH TO YOUR FLOWER.

7 Work the roses (4) in woven circle stitch with DMC pearl cotton size 5 color 352.

8 Work the large flower in backstitch with DMC cotton floss color 3832 and the long stem of the flower in backstitch with DMC Diamant metallic thread color D301.

9 Work the papa elephant's crown in straight stitch with DMC Diamant metallic thread color D301.

10 Embroider the bunting, working the outline of each flag in stem stitch and filling the inside using straight stitch with DMC cotton floss colors 17, 3835, 3853, 3846, 16, and 3839.

11 Work the string in straight stitch with DMC Diamant metallic thread color D301.

12 Work a French knot at each end of the bunting using DMC embroidery floss color 3832.

13 Work the little hearts in backstitch with DMC cotton floss color 3846.

14 Work the cheeks of the elephants in French knot with DMC pearl cotton size 5 color 352.

VARIATION: ELEPHANT LOVE

Illustration by Marie Savart Illustrations

What a pretty declaration of love by these two elephants, looking into each other's eyes from their separate hoops! A perfect project for beginners, this design is very easy and quick to embroider. In a child's room, above a bed or a crib, they will sweetly and endearingly watch over your little ones.

MATERIALS

- 2 linen squares, 16 x 16 in. (40 x 40 cm)
- Two 14 in. (35 cm) embroidery hoops
- Embroidery needle
- Embroidery pen

STITCHES USED

- Stem stitch (p. 10)
- Backstitch (p. 9)
- Straight stitch (p. 10)
- French knot (p. 11)
- Chain stitch (p. 12)

THREAD USED

DMC Pearl Cotton size 5

666 754

796

DMC Pearl Cotton size 8

413

DMC Satin Floss

S310

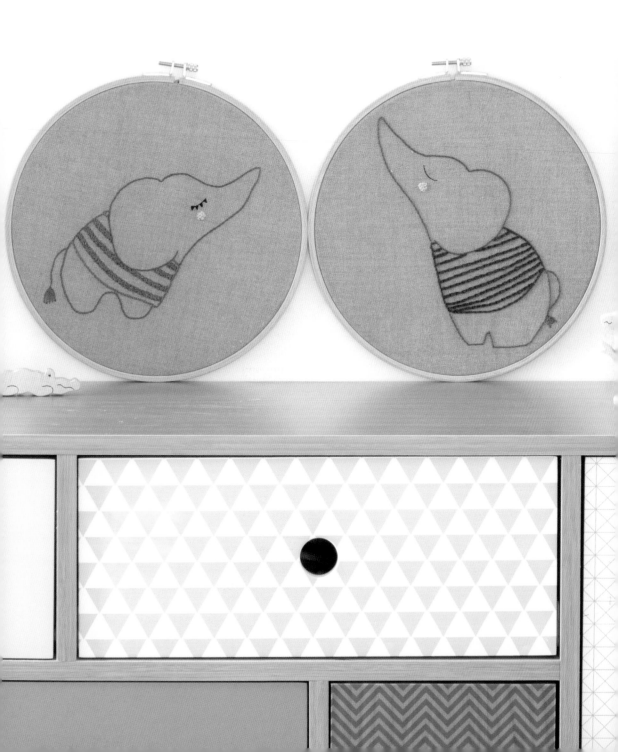

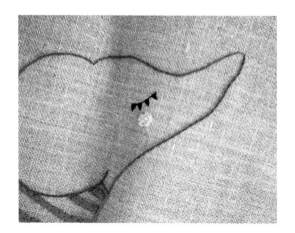

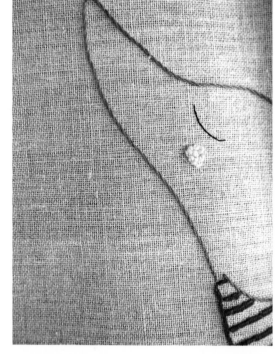

✕ INSTRUCTIONS

1 Transfer the illustration onto your fabric with the embroidery pen and place the fabric in your hoop.

2 Work the bodies and tails of the elephants in stem stitch with DMC pearl cotton size 8 color 413.

3 Work the eyes in backstitch and the eyelashes in straight stitch with DMC satin floss color S310.

4 Make the cheeks with French knots using DMC pearl cotton size 5 color 754.

5 Make the blue Breton shirt, working the outside edge in stem stitch and the stripes in chain stitch with DMC pearl cotton size 5 color 796.

6 Make the red Breton shirt, working the outside edge in stem stitch and the stripes in straight stitch with DMC pearl cotton size 5 color 666.

This template is shown at 70 percent of
its actual size. If you wish to embroider
it as is, use an 8 in. (20 cm) hoop.

FRENCH KNOT MINIATURES

Illustration by Charlotte & the Teapot

The French knot is a pretty embroidery stitch that gives depth and texture to your work. Here, we created larger knots by wrapping the thread around the needle several times for a very loopy, curly look. Have fun making these miniatures. They would be perfect made into pins, embroidered on your favorite denim jacket, or hanging on a wall in little colored hoops.

MATERIALS

- Linen, 6 x 6 in. (15 x 15 cm)
- 5 in. (12.5 cm) embroidery hoop
- Embroidery needle
- Beading needle
- Miyuki Delica 11/0 beads, Color DB0035 (galvanized silver)
- Embroidery pen

STITCHES USED

- Stem stitch (p. 10)
- Backstitch (p. 9)
- French knot (p. 11)
- Long and short satin stitch (p. 10)
- Straight stitch (p. 10)

THREAD USED

DMC Pearl Cotton size 5

937

DMC Pearl Cotton size 8

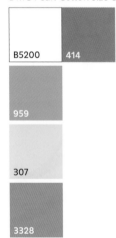

B5200

414

959

307

3328

Moon and Cloud

1 Transfer the illustration onto your fabric using the embroidery pen and place it in the hoop.

2 Work the outline of the moon in stem stitch with DMC pearl cotton size 8 color 307.

3 Work the outline of the star in backstitch using the same thread.

4 Fill the inside of the moon and the star with French knots using the same thread.

5 Work the outline of the cloud in stem stitch with DMC pearl cotton size 8 color 959.

6 Fill the inside of the cloud with French knots using DMC pearl cotton size 8 color 959.

Star, Moon, and Rainbow

1 Transfer the illustration onto your fabric using the embroidery pen and place it in the hoop.

2 Work the moon and the star in French knot using DMC pearl cotton size 8 color 307.

3 Work the rainbow in backstitch. For the inside bow use DMC pearl cotton size 8 color 307, for the middle bow use DMC pearl cotton size 8 color 959, and for the outside bow use DMC pearl cotton size 8 color 3328.

Bring the needle up from the wrong side to the right side of your work.

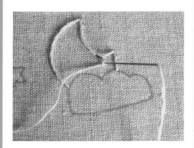

Wind thread around the needle. For a classic French knot, it is only wound around the needle one time. Here, to give more texture and a curly effect, wind the thread around the needle three times.

Pull gently on the thread to tighten, bringing the three loops formed to the bottom of the needle. Insert the needle through the fabric near the same spot, making sure the loops don't come off the needle.

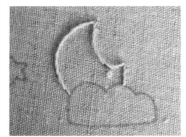

Here is your first knot. Repeat these steps until the area to be embroidered is covered.

Mountains

1 Transfer the illustration onto your fabric using the embroidery pen and place it in the hoop.

2 Stitch a silver Miyuki bead on each dot.

3 Starting at the base of the mountain, work the outline in backstitch and the inside in long and short satin stitch with DMC pearl cotton size 5 color 937.

4 For the snowy peaks, work the outlines in stem stitch and the inside in French knot, following the method shown on the preceding page, using DMC pearl cotton size 8 color B5200.

5 Stitch Miyuki beads on the little lines above the mountain.

Shooting Star

1 Transfer the illustration onto your fabric using the embroidery pen and place it in the hoop.

2 Work the tail of the star in straight stitch with leftover pieces of thread. Here we used DMC pearl cotton size 8 colors 3328, 959, 307, and 414.

3 For the star, work the outline in backstitch and the inside in French knot using DMC pearl cotton size 8 color 307.

MY EMBROIDERED JEWELRY

Illustrations by Frimouss

We are now seeing a trend in handcrafted jewelry, so why not transform your embroidery into pins? It is the best idea when you don't know what to do with your pretty embroidered designs. It's very easy and so original!

MATERIALS

- Linen, 10 x 10 in.
  (25 x 25 cm)
- Felt
- Water-soluble stabilizer
- Double-sided fusible
  webbing
- 8 in. (20 cm) embroidery
  hoop
- Embroidery needle

STITCHES USED

- Straight stitch (p. 10)
- Backstitch (p. 9)
- Stem stitch (p. 10)
- Long and short satin
  stitch (p. 10)

THREAD USED

DMC Six-Strand Cotton Embroidery Floss

3847   3851

Monstera Leaf

1 Transfer the illustration onto the water-soluble stabilizer and hold it firmly against the fabric with the hoop.

2 Work the outline of the leaf and its center in stem stitch with DMC cotton floss color 3847.

3 Work the inside of the leaf in long and short satin stitch with DMC cotton floss color 3851.

Palm Branch

1 Transfer the illustration onto the water-soluble stabilizer and hold it firmly against the fabric with the hoop.

2 Work the outline of the palm branch in backstitch with DMC cotton floss color 3847.

3 Work the inside of the leaves in straight stitch with the same floss.

4 To make your embroidery into pins, see the directions for the Archibald pin (p. 42), starting with step 4.

MY DARLING, MY DEER

Illustrations by Camille Isaac Caudeelice

These trompe-l'oeil deer play with outlines, silhouettes, and filled spaces using very colorful floral motifs. Worked almost exclusively in straight stitch, this embroidery pattern looks like fabric coloring pages!

MATERIALS

- 2 linen squares, 20 x 20 in. (50 x 50 cm)
- Two 16 in. (40 cm) embroidery hoops
- Embroidery needle

STITCHES USED

- Straight stitch (p. 10)
- Backstitch (p. 9)
- French knot (p. 11)

THREAD USED

DMC Pearl Cotton size 5

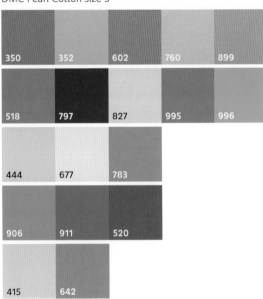

350 | 352 | 602 | 760 | 899
518 | 797 | 827 | 995 | 996
444 | 677 | 783
906 | 911 | 520
415 | 642

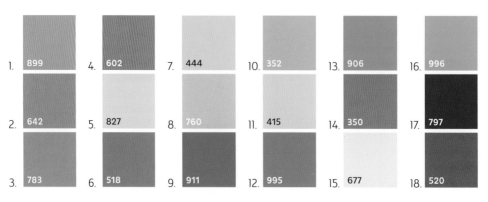

1.	899	4.	602	7.	444	10.	352	13.	906	16.	996
2.	642	5.	827	8.	760	11.	415	14.	350	17.	797
3.	783	6.	518	9.	911	12.	995	15.	677	18.	520

My Darling, My Deer

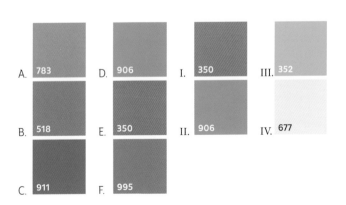

A.	783	D.	906	I.	350	III.	352
B.	518	E.	350	II.	906	IV.	677
C.	911	F.	995				

╳ INSTRUCTIONS

1 Work sections 1 to 18 in straight stitch.

2 Work parts A to F in backstitch.

3 Work sections I to IV in French knot.

N O T E

╳

IT IS SOMETIMES DIFFICULT TO FOLLOW THE LINES TRACED FROM
THE PATTERN TEMPLATE WHEN THERE ARE MANY DESIGN DETAILS,
AS IS THE CASE HERE. YOU CAN ALWAYS ALLOW YOURSELF TO
IMPROVISE, MAKING YOUR WORK UNIQUE.

This template is shown at 80 percent of its actual size. If you wish to embroider it as is, use a 10 in. (25 cm) hoop.

THREE LITTLE HOUSES

Illustration by Charlotte & the Teapot

This Flemish-style design is very original and would be lovely on a small bag, for example. You always need a little pouch to bring everywhere, and how satisfying to have made it yourself! Get started, and it won't be long before your friends want their own.

MATERIALS

- Linen, 16 in. x 10 in. (40 x 25 cm)
- 10 in. (25 cm) embroidery hoop
- Water-soluble stabilizer
- Embroidery needle

STITCHES USED

- Backstitch (p. 9)
- Straight stitch (p. 10)
- Stem stitch (p. 10)
- French knot (p. 11)

THREAD USED

DMC 6-Strand Cotton Embroidery Floss

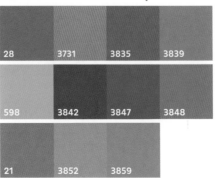

28 | 3731 | 3835 | 3839
598 | 3842 | 3847 | 3848
21 | 3852 | 3859

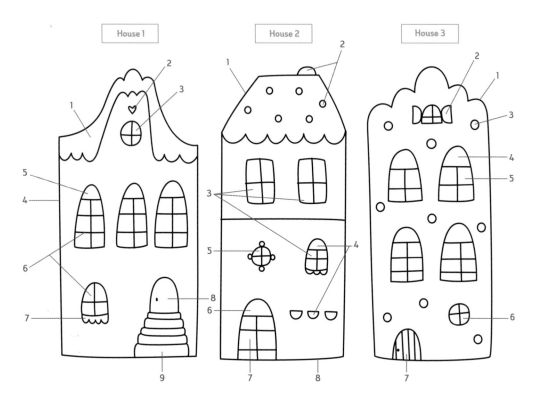

House 1

1 Transfer the illustration onto the water-soluble stabilizer and hold it firmly against the fabric with the hoop.

2 Work the outlines of the roof (1) in backstitch, and then work the interior of the roof in straight stitch with DMC cotton floss color 3847.

3 Work the heart (2) in straight stitch with DMC cotton floss color 3859.

4 Work the window grids (6) in backstitch with DMC cotton floss color 3842.

5 Work the outline of the house (4) in stem stitch with DMC cotton floss color 28.

6 Work the top of the three center windows (5) in straight stitch with DMC cotton floss color 598.

7 Work the gutter under the window (7) in straight stitch with DMC cotton floss color 3731.

8 Work the door (8) in backstitch with DMC cotton floss color 21. Make the handle with a French knot using the same thread.

9 Work the stairs in backstitch with DMC cotton floss color 3852.

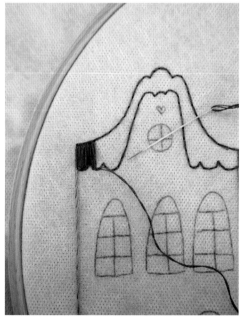

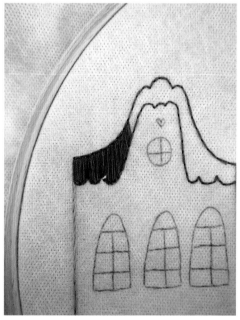

House 2

1 Work the outlines of the roof (1) in backstitch with DMC cotton floss color 3835.

2 Work the chimney and the dots on the roof (2) in straight stitch with DMC cotton floss color 3731.

3 Work the outline of the house (8) in stem stitch with DMC cotton floss color 598.

4 On the round window (5), work the outline in backstitch and the circles in French knot with DMC cotton floss color 3839.

5 Work the remaining windows (3) in backstitch with DMC cotton floss color 28.

6 Work the top of the lower right window and the half-circle motifs (4) in straight stitch with DMC cotton floss color 28.

7 Work the top of the door (6) in straight stitch with DMC cotton floss color 28.

8 Work the door (7) in backstitch with DMC cotton floss color 3842.

House 3

1 Work the outline of the house (1) in stem stitch with DMC cotton floss color 21.

2 Work the shutters (2) in straight stitch with DMC cotton floss color 3848.

3 Work the dots (3) in straight stitch with DMC cotton floss color 3852.

4 Work the top of the windows (4) in straight stitch with DMC cotton floss color 28.

5 Work all the windows (5) in backstitch with DMC cotton floss color 3842.

6 Work the round window (6) in backstitch with DMC cotton floss color 3848.

7 Work the door (7) in backstitch with DMC cotton floss color 3835. Make the door handle with a French knot using the same thread.

NATIVE AMERICAN HEADDRESS

Illustration by the author

How about giving your denim jacket a touch of rock and roll?
Make this cross-stitch Native American headdress and attach it to the back of your jacket.
You will definitely look and feel younger!

MATERIALS

- Aida cloth, 12 x 12 in.
  (30 x 30 cm)
- Piece of double-sided
  fusible webbing
- Embroidery needle

STITCHES USED

- Cross-stitch (p. 11)
- Backstitch (p. 9)

THREAD USED

DMC 6-Strand Cotton Embroidery Floss

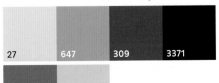

| 27 | 647 | 309 | 3371 |

| 163 | 3761 |

| 725 | 3778 |

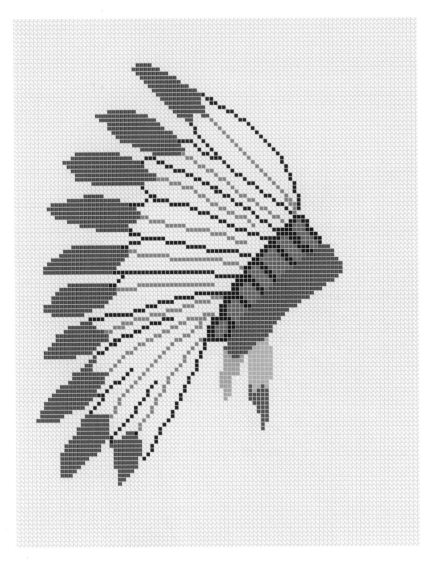

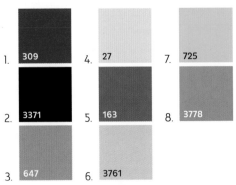

1. 309   4. 27   7. 725

2. 3371   5. 163   8. 3778

3. 647   6. 3761

× INSTRUCTIONS

1 Following the diagram and the color coding, work one cross-stitch for each square.

2 Once you have completed the embroidery, iron it with a damp pressing cloth.

3 Place the double-sided fusible webbing on the wrong side of your piece of embroidery and press with a warm iron to adhere.

4 Cut around the headdress as close as possible to the embroidery.

5 Iron your embroidery to the jacket to attach. For cleaner edges, you can backstitch all the way around the outer edge after attaching it to the denim jacket.

TIP

×

YOU MAY WISH TO OUTLINE THE EDGE OF THE FEATHERS AND THE
HEADBAND IN BACKSTITCH USING GOLD DMC DIAMANT METALLIC
THREAD. WHEN WORKING THE OUTLINE, INSERT THE NEEDLE IN
EVERY HOLE TO CREATE VERY EVEN STITCHING. THIS WILL MAKE
YOUR FINISHED WORK LOOK EVEN BETTER.

POPPY

Illustration by Atelier Sauvage

The poppy is a flower full of paradoxes that make it so appealing.
Despite its frail and fragile appearance, it grows everywhere; even though its petals
are robust enough to withstand the wind, it fades as soon as it is picked.
Capture this poppy in the style of a still life or botanical drawing.

MATERIALS

- Linen, 8 x 8 in. (20 x
  20 cm)
- Water-soluble stabilizer
- 6 in. (15 cm) embroidery
  hoop
- Embroidery needle

STITCHES USED

- Stem stitch (p. 10)
- Backstitch (p. 9)
- Straight stitch (p. 10)

THREAD USED

DMC 6-Strand Cotton Embroidery Floss

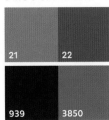

× INSTRUCTIONS

1 Work the outline of the petals in stem stitch with DMC cotton floss color 22.

2 Work the lines in the petals in backstitch with DMC cotton floss color 21.

3 Work the stem in stem stitch with DMC cotton floss color 939.

4 Work the center of the flower in straight stitch with DMC cotton floss color 939.

5 Work the leaf in backstitch with DMC cotton floss color 3850.

A MAGICAL WORLD

×

Illustration by Marie Savart Illustrations

Sweetness, gentleness, poetry, colors. A magical world represents everything that fills a child with wonder. Unicorns, stars, and rainbows bring the opportunity to play with colors and embroidery stitches and to use metallic threads that will give shine and depth to your work.

MATERIALS

- Linen, 16 x 16 in.
  (40 x 40 cm)
- Water-soluble stabilizer
- 14 in. (35 cm) embroidery
  hoop
- Embroidery needle

STITCHES USED

- Backstitch (p. 9)
- Straight stitch (p. 10)
- Stem stitch (p. 10)
- French knot (p. 11)

THREAD USED

DMC 6-Strand Cotton Embroidery Floss

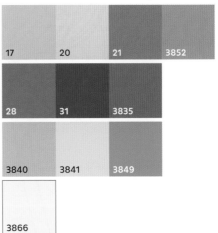

17	20	21	3852
28	31	3835	
3840	3841	3849	
3866			

Au Ver à Soie Braided Metallic Thread size 4

| 005 | 221 |

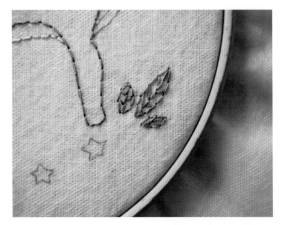

✕ INSTRUCTIONS

1 Transfer the illustration onto the water-soluble stabilizer and hold it firmly against the fabric with the hoop.

2 Outline the bodies of the two unicorns in backstitch with DMC cotton floss color 28.

3 Work the belly of the unicorns in backstitch with DMC cotton floss color 20.

4 Work the outline of the leaves and the veins in backstitch with DMC cotton floss color 3849.

5 For the stars, work the outline in backstitch and the inside in straight stitch with DMC cotton floss color 17.

6 Work the mane and the tail of the unicorns in backstitch with Au Ver à Soie size 4 braided metallic thread color 221.

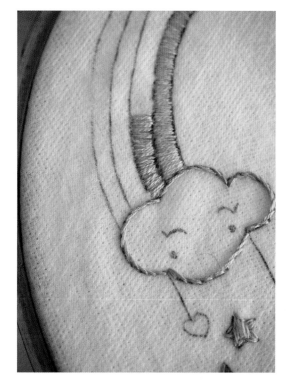

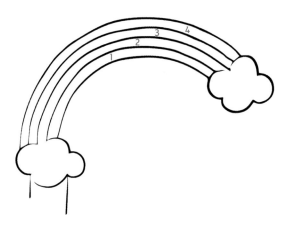

7 Work the horn of the unicorns in backstitch with DMC cotton floss color 21.

8 Embroider the large stars using the same method as for the small ones. Work the outline in backstitch and the inside in straight stitch with DMC cotton floss color 3852.

9 Work the outline of the clouds in stem stitch with DMC cotton floss color 3840.

10 Work the rainbow in straight stitch with DMC cotton floss color 20 for the first stripe (1), color 3841 for the second stripe (2), color 17 for the third stripe (3), and color 3849 for the fourth stripe (4).

11 Work the outside edges of the rainbow in stem stitch with DMC cotton floss color 3866.

12 Work all the hearts in straight stitch with DMC cotton floss color 20.

13 To embroider the wings of the small unicorn, work the inside in straight stitch with DMC cotton floss color 3840 and the outlines in backstitch with DMC cotton floss color 3835.

14 Work the wings of the large unicorn in backstitch with DMC cotton floss color 3840 for the base of the wing (1), color 31 for the first row of feathers (2), color 21 for the second row of feathers (3), and color 3835 for the last feathers (4).

15 Work the cheeks on the clouds and the unicorns in French knot with DMC cotton floss color 20.

16 Work the inside of the ear on the large unicorn in backstitch with DMC cotton thread color 20.

17 Work the eyes on the clouds and the unicorns in backstitch with the Au Ver à Soie size 4 braided metallic thread color 005.

18 Use straight stitch to add the threads from which the hearts are hanging with DMC cotton floss color 3841.

VARIATION: UNICORN

Illustration by Marie Savart Illustrations

This illustration by Marie, so sweet and delicate, is a real pleasure to embroider.
Play with the colors or add touches of shiny thread to make it unique and
give it a bit of magic.

MATERIALS

- Linen, 16 x 16 in. (40 x 40 cm)
- 14 in. (35 cm) embroidery hoop
- Embroidery needle
- Embroidery pen

STITCHES USED

- Stem stitch (p. 10)
- French knot (p. 11)
- Backstitch (p. 9)

THREAD USED

DMC 6-Strand Cotton Embroidery Floss

DMC Pearl Cotton size 8

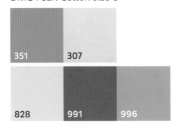

DMC Pearl Cotton size 12

DMC Metallic Pearl Cotton

✕ INSTRUCTIONS

1 Transfer the illustration onto your fabric using the embroidery pen and place it in the hoop.

2 Embroider the body in stem stitch with DMC pearl cotton size 12 color 932.

3 Work the belly and the inside of the ear in stem stitch with DMC pearl cotton size 12 color 316.

4 Use a French knot to make the cheek with DMC pearl cotton size 12 color 316.

5 Work the eyes in backstitch using a single strand of DMC cotton floss color 3799.

6 Work the horn in stem stitch using four strands of DMC metallic pearl cotton color 5282.

7 Work the tail and the mane in stem stitch following the color diagram on the next page.

Variation: Unicorn

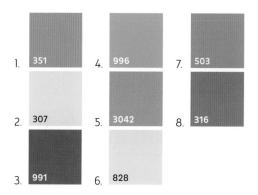

1.	351	4.	996	7.	503
2.	307	5.	3042	8.	316
3.	991	6.	828		

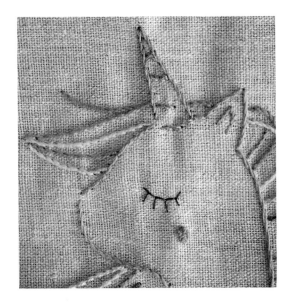

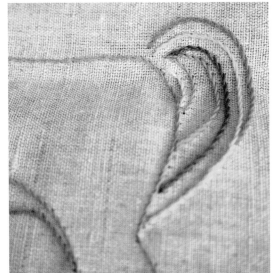

This template is shown at 80 percent of its actual size. If you wish to embroider it as is, use a 10 in. (25 cm) hoop.

PEACOCK!

Illustration by Camille Isaac Gaudeelier

We are used to keeping the different facets of fiber arts separate. For embroidery, we use embroidery thread and that's it. But have you ever tried to use another type of thread? Another material? To make the body of this peacock, I suggest using a fine fingering weight yarn to give your work texture and play up the contrasts. When you see the results, you will no longer look at your knitting yarns in the same way, and you will have no trouble imagining them in your future embroidery projects.

MATERIALS

- Linen, 12 x 12 in. (30 x 30 cm)
- Water-soluble stabilizer
- 10 in. (25 cm) embroidery hoop
- Embroidery needle
- Beading needle
- Miyuki beads

STITCHES USED

- Backstitch (p. 9)
- Straight stitch (p. 10)

THREAD USED

DMC 6-Strand Cotton Embroidery Floss

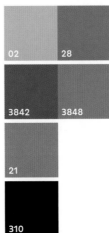

02   28
3842   3848
21
310

Phildar Partner Baby yarn

Curaçao

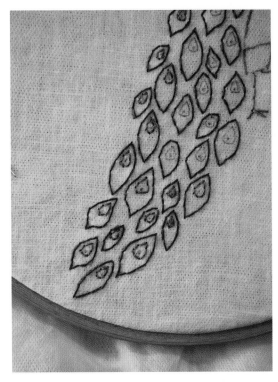

✕ INSTRUCTIONS

1 Transfer the illustration onto the water-soluble stabilizer and hold it firmly against the fabric with the hoop.

2 Work the large diamond shapes that make up the tail in backstitch with DMC cotton floss color 3842.

3 Work the small diamond shapes in backstitch with DMC cotton floss color 3848.

4 With your beading needle, stitch a Miyuki bead in the middle of each small diamond.

5 Work the legs in backstitch with DMC cotton floss color 21.

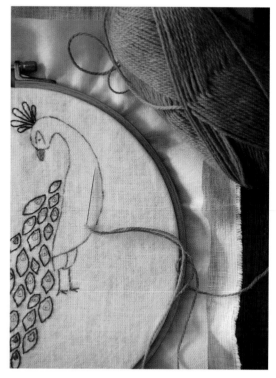

6 For the thighs, work the outlines in backstitch with DMC cotton floss color 28 and then the inside in straight stitch with DMC cotton floss color 02.

7 Work the beak in straight stitch with DMC cotton floss color 21.

8 Work the crest in backstitch with DMC cotton floss color 3842.

9 Work the eyebrow in backstitch with DMC cotton floss color 310. Using the same thread, make the eye with a French knot.

10 Embroider the body with the yarn. Cover the entire surface of the body by working short straight stitches in all directions to give a textured effect to the peacock's body. If needed, use a needle with a larger eye.

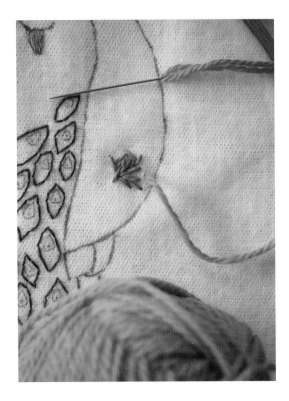

Peacock!

FLOWERS AND SEQUINS

Illustration by Charlotte & the Teapot

Sequins are so pretty used in embroidery! All of their facets reflect the light and give your work a touch of originality. If there is some hesitation about embroidering with sequins, it's often because we don't know how to use them. I suggest using them here to create oval frames around the flowers drawn by Charlotte. An effect both Slavic and retro!

MATERIALS

- Linen, 6 x 6 in. (15 x 15 cm) for each design
- Water-soluble stabilizer
- 6 in. (15 cm) embroidery hoop
- Embroidery needle
- Sequins

STITCHES USED

- Backstitch (p. 9)
- Straight stitch (p. 10)
- French knot (p. 11)

THREAD USED

DMC 6-Strand Cotton Embroidery Floss

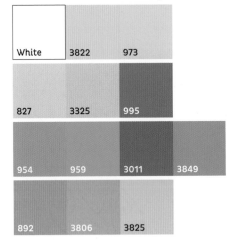

White	3822	973
827	3325	995
954	959	3011	3849
892	3806	3825

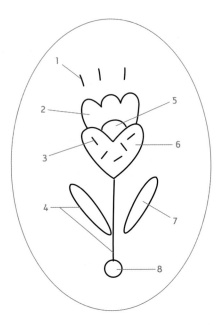

The numbers indicated in this illustration correspond to the numbers in parentheses found in the instructions.

Pink Flower

1 Transfer the illustration onto the water-soluble stabilizer and hold it firmly against the fabric with the hoop.

2 Work the outlines of the leaves and stem (4) in backstitch, with DMC cotton floss color 3011.

3 Work the inside of the leaves (7) in straight stitch with DMC cotton floss color 954.

4 Work the base (8) in straight stitch with DMC cotton floss color 3011.

5 Work the petal in the foreground (6) in straight stitch with the white DMC cotton floss.

6 Add the little lines across the petal (3) in straight stitch with DMC cotton floss color 959.

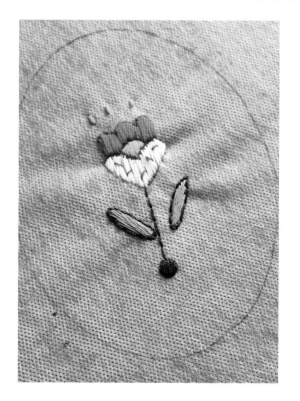

7   Work the center of the flower (5) in straight stitch with DMC cotton floss color 973.

8   Work the petal in the back (2) in straight stitch with DMC cotton floss color 3806.

9   Add the little lines above the flower (1) in straight stitch with DMC cotton floss color 973.

10 Embroider the oval with sequins as explained on page 138.

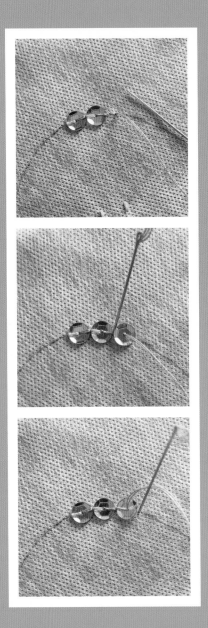

Bring the needle up from the wrong side to the right side of your work.

Thread a sequin over the needle and then bring the needle down at the left edge of the sequin.

Bring the needle back up at the center of the sequin and then bring it down again at the right edge of the sequin. Continue in this manner until the oval is completed.

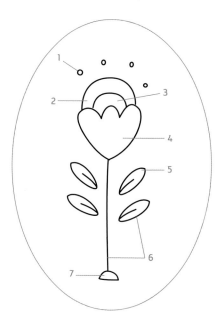

The numbers indicated in this illustration correspond to the numbers in parentheses found in the instructions.

Blue Flower

1 Transfer the illustration onto the water-soluble stabilizer and hold it firmly against the fabric with the hoop.

2 Work the outlines of the leaves and stem (6) in backstitch with DMC cotton floss color 3011. Work the base (7) in straight stitch with the same thread.

3 Work the inside of the leaves (5) in straight stitch with DMC cotton floss color 954.

4 Work the petal in the foreground (4) in straight stitch with DMC cotton floss color 3849.

5 Work the center of the flower (3) in straight stitch with the white DMC cotton floss.

6 Work the petal in the background (2) in straight stitch with DMC cotton floss color 3325.

7 Add the little dots above the flower (1) in French knot with DMC cotton floss color 892.

8 Embroider the oval with sequins as explained on page 138.

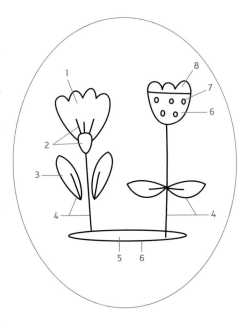

The numbers indicated in this illustration correspond to the numbers in parentheses found in the instructions.

The Two Flowers

1 Transfer the illustration onto the water-soluble stabilizer and hold it firmly against the fabric with the hoop.

2 Work the outlines of the leaves and stems (4) in backstitch with DMC cotton floss color 3011. Work the outline of the base (6) in straight stitch with the same thread.

3 Work the inside of the base (5) in straight stitch with DMC cotton floss color 827.

4 Work the base of the small flower (2) in straight stitch with DMC cotton floss color 973.

5 Work the petals of the small flower (1) in straight stitch with the white DMC cotton floss.

6 Add the little lines radiating from the base of the little flower (2) in straight stitch with DMC cotton floss color 973.

7 Work the base of the large flower (6) in straight stitch with DMC cotton floss color 3822.

8 Add the little dots on the large flower (7) in French knot with DMC cotton floss color 3825.

9 Work the petals of the large flower (8) in straight stitch with DMC cotton floss color 995.

10 Embroider the oval with sequins as explained on page 138.

Flowers and Sequins

MY CAT

Illustration by Charlotte & the Teapot

How calming is this little cat asleep in the yard! A few embroidery stitches, with some cheery colors, and he brightens up a dishtowel, an apron, or a tote bag.

MATERIALS

- Linen, 16 x 16 in. (40 x 40 cm)
- 14 in. (35 cm) embroidery hoop
- Embroidery needle
- Embroidery pen

STITCHES USED

- Stem stitch (p. 10)
- Backstitch (p. 9)
- Straight stitch (p. 10)
- French knot (p. 11)

THREAD USED

DMC Pearl Cotton size 5

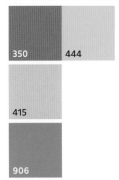

350 444

415

906

DMC Pearl Cotton size 8

413 828

DMC Pearl Cotton size 12

316

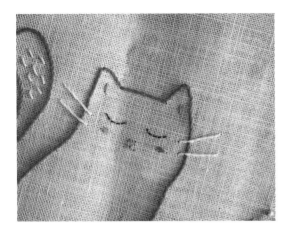

✕ INSTRUCTIONS

1 Transfer the illustration onto your fabric using the embroidery pen and place it in the hoop.

2 Embroider the body of the cat in stem stitch with DMC pearl cotton size 5 color 350.

3 Work the eyes in backstitch with DMC pearl cotton size 8 color 413.

4 Work the whiskers in stem stitch with DMC pearl cotton size 8 color 828.

5 Add the claws and the markings on the tail in straight stitch with DMC pearl cotton size 5 color 415.

6 Stitch the nose, cheeks, and ears in straight stitch with DMC pearl cotton size 12 color 316.

7 Work the leaves, grass, and stems in backstitch with DMC pearl cotton size 5 color 906. Work the inside of the large leaf in straight stitch.

8 Work the flowers in straight stitch with DMC pearl cotton size 5 color 444.

9 Use French knots to make the seeds with DMC pearl cotton size 5 color 415.

This template is shown at 70 percent of its actual size. If you wish to embroider it as is, use an 8 in. (20 cm) hoop.

MY CABINET OF CURIOSITIES

Illustration by Camille Isaac Caudrelier

Who has not been fascinated by collectors' cases where tiny creatures, one more colorful than the other, are exhibited? Make your own cabinet of curiosities by embroidering these insects. Have fun reproducing them in all different colors, displaying a large number of them in hoops of all shapes and sizes. They will give your space the look of an entomologist's office!

MATERIALS

- Linen, 6 x 6 in. (15 x 15 cm) for each design
- 6 in. (15 cm) hoop
- Embroidery needle
- Embroidery pen

STITCHES USED

- Backstitch (p. 9)
- Straight stitch (p. 10)
- Long and short satin stitch (p. 10)
- French knot (p. 11)
- Stem stitch (p. 10)

THREAD USED

DMC Pearl Cotton size 8

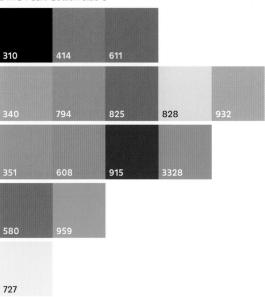

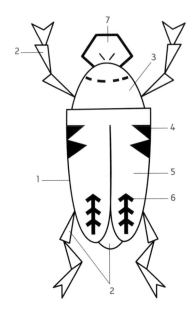

The numbers indicated in this illustration correspond to the numbers in parentheses found in the instructions.

Cockroach

1   Transfer the illustration onto your fabric with the embroidery pen and place it in the hoop.

2   Work the outlines of the insect (1) in backstitch with DMC pearl cotton size 8 color 310.

3   Work the inside of the legs and the lower abdomen (2) in straight stitch with DMC pearl cotton size 8 color 825.

4   Work the side markings (4) in straight stitch with DMC pearl cotton size 8 color 959.

5   Add the design on the bottom of the wings (6) in backstitch with DMC pearl cotton size 8 color 611.

6   Work the wings (5) in long and short satin stitch with DMC pearl cotton size 8 color 794.

7   Work the head (3) in straight stitch with DMC pearl cotton size 8 color 580.

8   Work the space between the antennae (7) in straight stitch with DMC pearl cotton size 8 color 340.

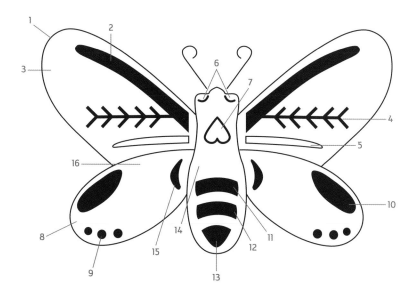

The numbers indicated in this illustration correspond to the numbers in parentheses found in the instructions.

Butterfly

1 Transfer the illustration onto your fabric with the embroidery pen and place it in the hoop.

2 Work the outlines of the butterfly (1) in backstitch with DMC pearl cotton size 8 color 310.

3 Work the heart (7) in French knot with DMC pearl cotton size 8 color 825.

4 Work the bands below the heart in straight stitch. Make the first band (11) with DMC pearl cotton size 8 color 3328, the second (12) with DMC pearl cotton size 8 color 727, and the third (13) with DMC pearl cotton size 8 color 959.

5 Work the body of the butterfly (14) in straight stitch with DMC pearl cotton size 8 color 580.

6 Add the motifs on the lower part of the wings. Work the half-moons (15) in straight stitch with DMC pearl cotton size 8 color 580, and then the ovals (10) in straight stitch with DMC pearl cotton size 8 color 932 and the three dots (9) in French knot with DMC pearl cotton size 8 color 727.

7 Work the lower part of the wings (16) in straight stitch with DMC pearl cotton size 8 color 959.

8 Add the motifs on the upper part of the wings. Work the bands on top (2) in straight stitch with DMC pearl cotton size 8 color 932 and the middle motif (4) in straight stitch with DMC pearl cotton size 8 color 959. For the last band (5), work the outline in stem stitch with DMC pearl cotton size 8 color 825 and the inside in straight stitch with DMC pearl cotton size 8 color 727.

9 Work the upper part of the wings (3) in straight stitch with DMC pearl cotton size 8 color 351.

10 Work the eyes (6) in straight stitch with DMC pearl cotton size 8 color 959.

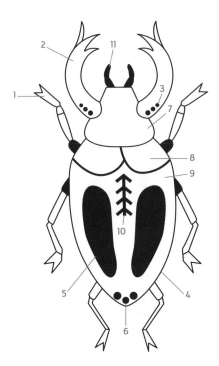

The numbers indicated in this illustration correspond to the numbers in parentheses found in the instructions.

Scarab Beetle

1 Transfer the illustration onto your fabric with the embroidery pen and place it in the hoop.

2 Work the outlines (4) in backstitch with DMC pearl cotton size 8 color 310.

3 Work the head (7) in straight stitch with DMC pearl cotton size 8 color 825.

4 Work the horns (2) in straight stitch with DMC pearl cotton size 8 color 959. Make the 3 dots (3) with French knots using DMC pearl cotton size 8 color 825.

5 Work the top part of the body (8) in straight stitch with DMC pearl cotton size 8 color 608.

6 Work the bands (5) in straight stitch with DMC pearl cotton size 8 color 580.

7 Work the center motif (10) in straight stitch with DMC pearl cotton size 8 color 414.

8 Make the three dots at the bottom of the body (6) with French knots using DMC pearl cotton size 8 color 351.

9 Work the body (9) in straight stitch with DMC pearl cotton size 8 color 828.

10 Work the inside of the legs (1) in straight stitch with DMC pearl cotton size 8 color 915.

11 Work the horns (11) in backstitch with DMC pearl cotton size 8 color 310.

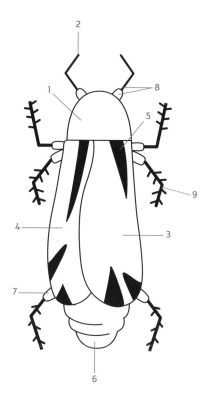

The numbers indicated in this illustration correspond to the numbers in parentheses found in the instructions.

Ground Beetle

1 Transfer the illustration onto your fabric with the embroidery pen and place it in the hoop.

2 Work the antennae (2), the legs (9) and the outline of the insect in backstitch with DMC pearl cotton size 8 color 310.

3 Work the head (1) in straight stitch with DMC pearl cotton size 8 color 959.

4 Work the top of the legs (7) in straight stitch with DMC pearl cotton size 8 color 727.

5 Work the eyes (8) in straight stitch with DMC pearl cotton size 8 color 932.

6 Work the right wing (3) in straight stitch with DMC pearl cotton size 8 color 414.

7 Work the left wing (4) in straight stitch with DMC pearl cotton size 8 color 932.

8 Work the abdomen (6) in straight stitch with DMC pearl cotton size 8 color 915.

9 Work the markings (5) in straight stitch with DMC pearl cotton size 8 color 825.

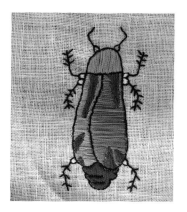

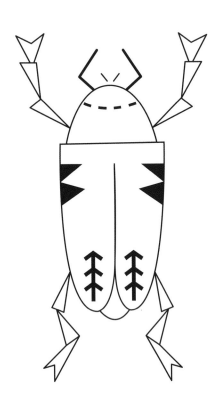

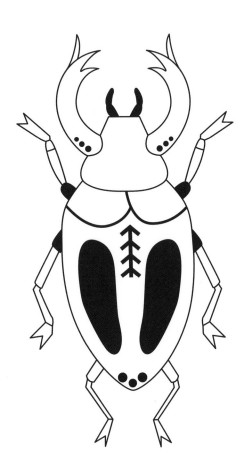

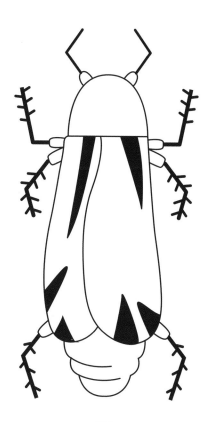

MELODY THE MERMAID

Illustration by Camille Isaac Gaudeclice

Miyuki beads are tiny glass beads that come from Japan. Unlike seed beads, they are all calibrated to be consistent in size so that they can be lined up in consistent patterns. Often used to make jewelry, they are also very pretty used in embroidery.

MATERIALS

- Linen, 12 x 12 in. (30 x 30 cm)
- 10 in. (25 cm) embroidery hoop
- Embroidery needle
- Beading needle
- Embroidery pen
- Miyuki Delica 11/0 beads, color 1496 (opaque light mint green)
- Miyuki Delica 11/0 beads, color 1831 (galvanized silver)
- Miyuki Delica 11/0 beads, color 2131 (opaque eucalyptus)
- Nylon thread

STITCHES USED

- Stem stitch (p. 10)
- Backstitch (p. 9)
- Straight stitch (p. 10)

THREAD USED

DMC 6-Strand Cotton Embroidery Floss

3799

DMC Pearl Cotton Size 5

318

DMC Pearl Cotton Size 8

351   825   912   991

DMC Pearl Cotton Size 12

932

DMC Metallic Pearl Cotton Size 5

5283

NOTE

BECAUSE THE MIYUKI BEADS HAVE A VERY SMALL HOLE SIZE, YOUR EMBROIDERY NEEDLE WILL NOT GO THROUGH THE BEAD. IT IS PREFERABLE TO EQUIP YOURSELF WITH A NEEDLE SPECIFICALLY DESIGNED FOR SEWING BEADS.

AMERIQUE
Tre de Baffin
Canal de Fox
Presq le de Melville
C. de Bootha
Tre du Roi Guillaume
Terre Victoria
Terre Wollaston
Presq le de Bootha
Esquimaux (Innuit)
Tre du Prince Guillaume
BAIE DE BAFFIN
I. Disko
Péninsule Nursoak
Fiord Omenak
I. Bylot
Somerset septental
Tre du Prince de Galles
Canal Mac Clintock
Tre du Prince Albert
Dét. de Lancastre
Dét. de Barrow
Upernivik
Tasiusak
Devon du Nd
I. Cornouaille
Winter Harbour
Tre de Banks
Baie de Franklin
C. Bathurst
Hivernage de Franklin 1845
I. Bathurst
Baie Melville
Grinnell
I. Melville
Dét. de Banks
Péninsule de Hayes
AND (D)
I. du Pce Patrick
20° 388 k
Is du Roi
Tre Alexandra
I. Northbrook
I. Mac-Clintock
I. Hall
ENTS
ARCTIQUE
GLACIAL
OCÉAN
I. Benne
I. Kotel
I. Belkov
Iles Liak
I. Stolbovyi
elle-Zemble (R)
C. du Désir
Be de Taïmyr
I. de la Solitude
C. Middendorf
I. Taïmyr
MER DE NORDENSKIŒLD
Khatanga
Delta de la Léna
MER DE KARA
I. Blanche
I. Dickson
Nordenskiœld
Presq le
Porte de Kara
I. Vaïgatch
Ile Sibiriakov
Péninsule des Samoyèdes ou de Ialmal
Golfe de l'Ob
Zverevo
Piasina R.
Anabara
Léna F.
Verkhoïa

× INSTRUCTIONS

1 Transfer the illustration onto your fabric with the embroidery pen and place it in the hoop.

2 Work the hair in stem stitch with DMC pearl cotton size 8 color 351.

3 Work the shells on the bust in backstitch with DMC pearl cotton size 8 color 825.

4 Work the outline of the mermaid's chest in backstitch using a single strand of DMC cotton floss color 3799.

5 Work the outline of the tail in stem stitch with DMC pearl cotton size 8 color 912 and the fins with DMC pearl cotton size 8 color 991.

6 Work the sea and the waves in stem stitch with DMC pearl cotton size 12 color 932.

7 Work the rock in stem stitch with DMC pearl cotton size 5 color 318.

8 Work the birds in straight stitch with DMC metallic pearl cotton size 5 color 5283.

9 Stitch the Miyuki beads onto the tail. They will represent scales.

TIP

STITCH ON THE THREE COLORS OF BEADS
RANDOMLY FOR A NATURAL LOOK.

EMBROIDERING WITH MIYUKI BEADS

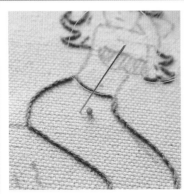

Thread the nylon thread onto your beading needle and make a small knot at the end.

Thread a bead onto the needle and sew it to the fabric.

Thread and sew on the beads one after the other without leaving much (if any) space between them until the entire tail is covered.

TRULY, MADLY, WILDLY

Illustration by Atelier Sauvage

The fine lines of a woman's silhouette, an eruption of flowers . . . this can only be an illustration by Clarisse. Enjoy embroidering this delicate design; play with the contrast between the outline of the woman, monochromatic and minimalist, and the explosion of colors in the floral motif.

MATERIALS

- Linen, 16 x 16 in. (40 x 40 cm)
- Water-soluble stabilizer
- 14 in. (35 cm) embroidery hoop
- Embroidery needle

STITCHES USED

- Backstitch (p. 9)
- Straight stitch (p. 10)
- French knot (p. 11)
- Fishbone stitch (p. 12)

THREAD USED

DMC 6-Strand Cotton Embroidery Floss

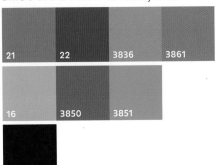

× INSTRUCTIONS

1 Transfer the illustration onto the water-soluble stabilizer and hold it firmly against the fabric with the hoop.

2 Work the outline of the silhouette in backstitch with DMC cotton floss color 939. Work the lips in straight stitch using a single strand from the skein.

3 Work the outlines of the three large flowers (1, 2, and 3) in backstitch with DMC cotton floss color 22. Work French knots in the center of flowers 1 and 3 with the same thread.

4 Work the interior of flower 1 in backstitch with DMC cotton floss color 21.

5 Work the interior of flower 2 in straight stitch with DMC cotton floss color 3836.

6 Work the interior of flower 3 in straight stitch with DMC cotton floss color 3861.

7 Work the outline of all the small flowers in backstitch with DMC cotton floss color 21. Work the center of the small flowers in French knot with the same thread.

8 Work the upper leaves (A) in fishbone stitch with DMC cotton floss color 3850.

9 Work the outline and veins of the largest leaf (B) in backstitch with DMC cotton floss color 3850 and the interior in straight stitch with DMC cotton floss color 3851.

10 Work the outlines and center veins of the small leaves (C) in backstitch with DMC cotton floss color 3850 and the interior in straight stitch with DMC cotton floss color 16.

11 Work the stems (D) in backstitch with DMC cotton floss color 3850.

The numbers and letters indicated in this illustration correspond to the numbers/letters in parentheses found in the instructions.

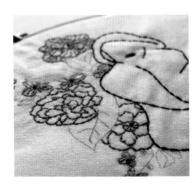

ATELIER SAUVAGE

My name is Clarisse Barde, and I am a professional notebook doodler with a longtime proclivity for drawing flowers. I have recently begun to share some of my designs on Instagram. Passionate about pretty things and little trifles, I like photography, going out for a drink at Bordeaux's outdoor bars, and customizing my clothes!

I started drawing pared-down illustrations on a graphics tablet with the idea of embroidering them. Finally, I was able to get out my thread and I just continued to imagine female silhouettes wildly covered in flowers.

 @ateliersauvage

CAMILLE ISAAC CAUDRELIER

Here are the nine things you should know about me. (Why nine? Ten is too expected. I could just as well have chosen twenty-seven, but that might get to be a bit too much!)

1. I was born on Saturday, February 27, 1988, at 10:30 p.m. On August 27, 2016, I went from a Miss to a Missus. Sentimental? Just a bit.

2. I am tall, and whoever says tall often says JTS syndrome = Jeans Too Short.

3. I need to work with my hands. I draw, I sew, I crochet, I embroider. I am what could be called a Jill-of-all-trades.

4. I cried watching the Intermarché commercial where the young boy decides to learn how to cook to charm the pretty cashier. Emotional much? A tad.

5. Speaking of love, one of the things I am most proud of is our DIY wedding— we thought of everything and made everything ourselves.

6. My job? Leading creative workshops for adults and children. Nice, right?

7. I am not very athletic. My last attempt at jogging goes back to 2012. My thighs still remember. . . .

8. I like to enjoy quiet times, watch the sunset, listen to the seagulls laugh, and simply breathe!

9. My favorite movie is the comedy *La Cité de la Peur*—an old horror movie parody!

If you enjoyed this, you can continue to follow my little journey on Instagram.

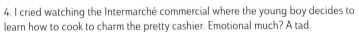

@camillou_isaac   @camilleetsesatelierscreatifs

CHARLOTTE & THE TEAPOT

A textile designer by training and based in Lyon, I offer my illustrations on different media (paper, fabric) through my little brand Charlotte & the Teapot, created after I finished my studies in 2015.

My illustrations are mainly inspired by animals and nature, my travels, and the world of childhood. I also draw poetic and imaginary scenes or simply objects and moments from daily life, in a style that is rather soft and sweet, dainty and feminine.

I also like to work with materials and create prints that will complement my collections, available on fabric to make pillows or other decorative items for the home.

My collections are intended for all who enjoy items from small, unique designers, who wish to offer ethical gifts to their loved ones, or even those who want an original decoration for a baby's or child's room.

I hope that you enjoy the designs created for this book, inspired by a little feline in its mountains and by one of my favorite cities, which is Amsterdam. If so, I invite you to discover more of my artistic world at my personal site: www.charlotteandtheteapot.com.

FRIMOUSS

I am Stéphanie Duvivier, alias Frimouss, a creative entrepreneur brimming with imagination, the rhythm of my days punctuated with a nice mix of humor, patience, and skill.

I am interested in and passionate about so many things, and engaged in many artistic endeavors, but those I am most fond of are engraving (I create personalized stamps that I engrave by hand and which can be used on paper, fabric, wood, leather, cardboard, etc.), gouache and watercolor illustrations (I paint portraits or sketches to decorate your walls), and sewing little characters like the cat Cramite or the bat Aglaé, who are adopted by my little (and bigger) clients. All my work can be seen on my Instagram account and my online shop at Etsy SDuvivier.

See you soon!

 @la-frimouss-sduvivier

MARIE SAVART ILLUSTRATIONS

A love story.

Creation and love . . . each new project is a marvelous source of inspiration.

I like to feel things. There is a story and especially emotions in everything, everywhere. I am sensitive to everything around me. All of these little nothings of daily life turn into a big everything. I relish this perpetually-being-renewed happiness by expressing my creativity in poetry, putting magnified moments of life into colors. I take the time to share the things I think, imagine, and draw.

Yes, projects are fussed over; every little line is a bit magical. My creations nourish my endless need to meet my emotions head-on and use them in productive ways.

You have the words. . . . Now I can't wait to sketch them and add some nuance.

I am Marie, thirty-four years old. Wife, mother, creator, entrepreneur, dreamer, lover—I am a thousand things. To know more, go to:

@mariesavartillustrations (Instagram)

Marie Savart illustrations (Facebook)
For a bit (or a lot) more . . . www.mariesavart.com